A Fine Opportunity Lost

JAMES LONGSTREET'S EAST TENNESSEE CAMPAIGN, NOVEMBER 1863–APRIL 1864

by Col. Ed Lowe (USA, Ret.)

EMERGING CIVIL WAR SERIES

Chris Mackowski, series editor
Cecily Nelson Zander, chief historian

The Emerging Civil War Series

offers compelling, easy-to-read overviews of some of the Civil War's most important battles and stories.

Recipient of the Army Historical Foundation's Lieutenant General Richard G. Trefry Award for contributions to the literature on the history of the U.S. Army

Also part of the Emerging Civil War Series:

All Hell Can't Stop Them: The Battles for Chattanooga: Missionary Ridge and Ringgold, November 24–27, 1863 by David A. Powell

Battle Above the Clouds: Lifting the Siege of Chattanooga and the Battle of Lookout Mountain, October 16–November 24, 1863 by David A. Powell

Bushwhacking on a Grand Scale: The Battle of Chickamauga, September 18–20, 1863 by William Lee White

Hell Itself: The Battle of the Wilderness, May 5–7, 1864 by Chris Mackowski

Don't Give an Inch: The Second Day at Gettysburg, July 2, 1863—From Little Round Top to Cemetery Ridge by Chris Mackowski, Kristopher D. White, and Daniel T. Davis

A Long and Bloody Task: The Atlanta Campaign from Dalton through Kennesaw to the Chattahoochee, May 5–July 18, 1864 by Stephen Davis

Never Such a Campaign: The Battle of Second Manassas, August 28–30, 1862 by Dan Welch and Kevin R. Pawlak

Race to the Potomac: Lee and Meade After Gettysburg, July 4–14, 1863 by Bradley M. and Linda I. Gottfried

Simply Murder: The Battle of Fredericksburg, December 13, 1862 by Chris Mackowski and Kristopher D. White

Stay and Fight It Out: The Second Day at Gettysburg, July 2, 1863—Culp's Hill and the Northern End of the Battlefield by Kristopher D. White and Chris Mackowski

For a complete list of titles in the Emerging Civil War Series, visit www.emergingcivilwar.com.

JAMES LONGSTREET'S EAST TENNESSEE CAMPAIGN, NOVEMBER 1863–APRIL 1864

by Col. Ed Lowe (USA, Ret.)

EMERGING CIVIL WAR SERIES

Savas Beatie
California

First edition, first printing

ISBN-13 (paperback): 978-1-61121-673-8
ISBN-13 (ebook): 978-1-61121-674-5

Library of Congress Control Number: 2023038040

Names: Lowe, Ed, 1967- author.
Title: A Fine Opportunity Lost: James Longstreet's East Tennessee Campaign, November 1863 - April 1864 / by COL (RET) Ed Lowe.
Other titles: James Longstreet's East Tennessee Campaign, November 1863 - April 1864
Description: El Dorado Hills, CA : Savas Beatie LLC, [2024] | Series: Emerging Civil War series | Summary: "Lieutenant General James Longstreet's deployment to East Tennessee promised a chance to shine. Reassigned to the Western Theater because of sliding fortunes there, the Old Warhorse hoped to run free with-finally-an independent command of his own. Unexpectedly, Longstreet and Burnside from the Eastern Theater now found themselves transplanted in the Western-familiar adversaries on unfamiliar ground. The fate of East Tennessee hung in the balance, and the reputations of the commanders would be won or lost"-- Provided by publisher.
Identifiers: LCCN 2023038040 | ISBN 9781611216738 (paperback) | ISBN 9781611216745 (ebook)
Subjects: LCSH: Longstreet, James, 1821-1904. | Tennessee, East--History--Civil War, 1861-1865. | Generals--Confederate States of America--Biography. | United States--History--Civil War, 1861-1865--Campaigns.
Classification: LCC E475.9 .L694 2023 | DDC 973.7/35--dc23/eng/20230905
LC record available at https://lccn.loc.gov/2023038040

Printed and bound in the United Kingdom

Published by
Savas Beatie LLC
989 Governor Drive, Suite 102
El Dorado Hills, California 95762
Phone: 916-941-6896
sales@savasbeatie.com
www.savasbeatie.com

Savas Beatie titles are available at special discounts for bulk purchases in the United States by corporations, institutions, and other organizations. For more details, you may e-mail us at sales@savasbeatie.com or visit our website at www.savasbeatie.com for additional information.

To my late father, Bob Lowe, and father-in-law, Jim Sheffer, for their wisdom, humor, and passion for the little things in life.

To my late brother-in-law, Phillip Sheffer, for his dedication and service to others, an example for all to emulate.

To my wife, Suzanne, for her endless encouragement and support through all the years. Priceless.

Table of Contents

Footnotes for this volume are available at
https://emergingcivilwar.com/publication/footnotes/

List of Maps

Maps by Hal Jespersen

PHOTO CREDITS: *A Photographic History of the Civil War* (aphcw); American Civil War Museum (acwm); Chris Mackowski (cm); Department of Veteran Affairs, National Cemetery Administration, History Program (va); Doug Scott (ds); Ed Lowe (el); Emerging Civil War (ecw); Gerald Augustus (ga); *Harper's Weekly* (hw); Indiana Historical Society (ihs); Jim Doncaster (jd); Library of Congress (loc); McClung Historical Collection (mhc); Mississippi Department of Archives and History (mdah); National Archives (na); National Park Service (nps); Scott Rogers (sr); Special Collections Library of the University of Tennessee, Knoxville (sclut); Tennessee Special Libraries Collection (tslc)

For the Emerging Civil War Series

Theodore P. Savas, *publisher*
Sarah Keeney, *editorial consultant*
Veronica Kane, *production supervisor*
David Snyder, *copyeditor*
Patrick McCormick, *proofreader*

Chris Mackowski, *series editor and co-founder*
Cecily Nelson Zander, *chief historian*
Kristopher D. White, *emeritus editor*

Design and layout by Jess Maxfield
Maps by Hal Jesperson

Acknowledgments

It was 2016, and I had retired from the U.S. Army after 26 years of active service, finding a home in Chattanooga, Tennessee. Though a lifelong student of military history and specifically the Civil War, my last military assignment was a stone's throw from Gettysburg, Pennsylvania, in Carlisle. My wife, Suzanne, and I spent hours in bed and breakfasts in the cozy battlefield town, and my time there sparked a flame: a more reflective interest in the Civil War. I gained a deep appreciation for Civil War historians and the stories they told.

Moving to Chattanooga, I came to know and respect historians associated with the Western Theater, such as Jim Ogden and Lee White from the Chickamauga and Chattanooga National Military Park. I came to read the time-honored works of Dave Powell and other authors such as Steven Woodworth for their contribution to the study of those battles.

An idea formed as Suzanne and I were looking for a more permanent home: a book that covered James

Longstreet's First Corps from Gettysburg through his East Tennessee Campaign. The idea came to life with a few chapters on the battle of Chickamauga. Submitting my proposal to Ted Savas, I was so pleased that he accepted my idea. I signed a contract and was off and running. As COVID impacted the editing process, I read more books in the Emerging Civil War Series and found them fascinating—quick reads, packed full of solid information. I pitched an idea to Chris Mackowski about an ECW book that focused on Longstreet's East Tennessee Campaign. He liked the idea, and here we are. I offer my gratitude to both Ted and Chris for taking a chance on a first-time author. Their patience and guidance proved so helpful. Also, to Hal Jespersen who produced the maps for my first work and filtered over to this smaller, compact book. I'm deeply appreciative to editors Leon Reed and Cecily Zander for their concise and meaningful recommendations, which only made the book more readable and enjoyable. Lastly, I want to

James Longstreet used this house, the Bleak House, as his headquarters during the assault on Knoxville. Today, the United Daughters of the Confederacy operate the building as a museum. (cm)

U. H. Buchtel of Company H, 104th Ohio, made the original image upon which this drawing was based. The image clearly shows the cotton bales, tree stumps, and wire entanglements, all used to complement the fort's defenses. (mhc)

thank my daughter Robyn for her timely editing of the photographs for the book.

As I dug deeper into my research for this book, I found the Longstreet Museum in Russellville, Tennessee. Pointing out some of the aspects of the campaign and highlights proved essential additions to this book, and I offer my thanks. I am also thankful to my friend Gerald Augustus and his wife, Sandra. They welcomed Suzanne and me into their home. Gerald drove us around the area of Loudon and Lenoir City, showing us some of the key sites from the war. Gerald also provided invaluable recommendations in an early draft of the book. I'm also grateful to Jim Doncaster of the Knoxville Civil War Round Table for providing an appendix on critical areas and preservation efforts around Knoxville.

I extend appreciation to members of our round table here in Chattanooga for their encouragement and support, including my dear friend, historian, author, and tour guide at Chickamauga and Chattanooga, Robert Carter. And though he's a Dodgers fan, I

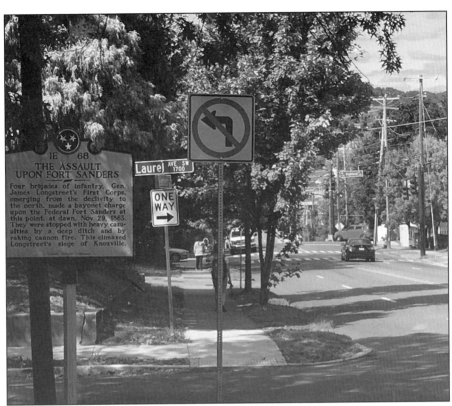

express my devotion to Skip Collinge for his passion for all things history. Both Robert and Skip have motivated me in many ways I can't properly articulate. It has also been a great joy participating in the round table in Chattanooga, sharing an appreciation of our local and national history.

Lastly, I must thank my wife, Suzanne, my two daughters, Robyn and Sarah, and son-in-law, Travis. They are truly the joy of my life. Suzanne was a fine editor and always there to bounce ideas off of, offering wonderful suggestions. She was most patient indeed. Finally, 1 Corinthians 10:31 says whatever we're to do, we're to do it for the Glory of God. So, to His Glory.

This view down South 17th Street looks down in the direction that Wofford's Brigade assaulted from, providing a good perspective of the elevation difference they had to overcome. (cm)

THE HANDS THAT ONCE WERE RAISED IN STRIFE
NOW CLASP A BROTHER'S HAND,
AND LONG AS FLOWS THE TIDE OF LIFE —
IN PEACE, IN TOIL, WHEN WAR IS RIFE —
WE SHALL AS BROTHER'S STAND,
ONE HEART, ONE SOUL FOR OUR FREE LAND.

J. I. C. CLARKE

Foreword

The monument to the 79th New York "Highlanders" Infantry Regiment in Knoxville emphasized postwar reconciliation. (cm)

No matter when you began your study of Civil War history—be it young or old—it does not take long before you notice that Confederate General James Longstreet is not only a major figure in the war, but that he is surrounded by controversy. Known as a gifted tactician, beloved by his men, respected by his officers, dedicated to his cause, and Robert E. Lee's second in command of the Army of Northern Virginia, Longstreet, nevertheless, was also purported to be rigidly stubborn, argumentative, and sulky. Longstreet fought from the beginning of the war, serving from the First Battle of Manassas to Appomattox. But, despite the thousands of words that have been written about the battles and Longstreet's involvement in them, large gaps in our knowledge of his service still need to be filled. In this book, *A Fine Opportunity Lost*, retired U.S. Army Col. Ed Lowe has ably filled one of those gaps.

Ed Lowe and I are avid battlefield trampers who share a great love of our nearest battlefield park, Chickamauga. We met after Ed retired from the army and settled in Tennessee. Over many years, our shared interest in "walking the ground" led to discussions about strategy, favorite regiments, decision making, tactics, and leadership. It soon became apparent to me that he had a profound interest in one of the Chickamauga and Chattanooga Campaign's most famous figures—Lt. Gen. James Longstreet. Ed's keen interest in Longstreet, his career-long insight into military leadership, coupled with his inquisitive nature and determination to uncover all the facts, makes him the ideal person to write this book.

By late July 1863, Longstreet was not a happy man. Although not outwardly showing it, his relationship with Lee had soured after the Battle of Gettysburg. Longstreet had disagreed with Lee about the strategy used in that campaign and the tactics employed once the battle was joined. Longstreet felt that his opinions should have carried more weight with Lee, and that he had had an agreement with Lee to fight a defensive battle once in enemy territory. Neither occurred. Later that summer when the idea was put forth to move troops from Lee's Army of Northern Virginia to Braxton Bragg's Army of Tennessee, Longstreet let it be known that he was willing to go.

Longstreet reported to Bragg's headquarters about 11:00 p.m. on September 19, 1863, after the second day of the bloody battle of Chickamauga. Influenced by Longstreet's stature as the second in command of the Army of Northern Virginia and by his immense reputation as a battlefield tactician, Bragg decided to overhaul the command structure of the Army of Tennessee in the middle of a major battle and appoint Longstreet as his Left Wing commander. The next day, the Army of Tennessee won a stunning victory over the mistake-laden Army of the Cumberland, in no small part because of Longstreet's involvement in the battle. The newly christened "Bull of the Woods" had lived up to his reputation.

But after the battle of Chickamauga, Longstreet's relationship with Bragg began to deteriorate. Never one to foster a harmonious relationship among his generals, Bragg bluntly, and without discussion, rebuffed Longstreet's suggestions for the recapture of Chattanooga. Unlike Lee, who encouraged discussion and fostered new ideas, Bragg wanted nothing to do with opinions he had determined would not work. It did not take long for the relationship between Bragg and Longstreet to descend to the level of most of Bragg's other chief subordinates—one of mistrust,

pettiness, exasperation, and paranoia. Longstreet soon sided with the group of generals who worked to remove Bragg from command of the Army of Tennessee. The long-festering issue of Braxton Bragg's command had now reached a roiling broil.

Confederate President Jefferson Davis's visit to the Army of Tennessee in early October 1863 settled the command issue in front of Chattanooga—Braxton Bragg would stay in command—but two of the three lieutenant generals serving with the army would be relieved. Leonidas Polk and Daniel Harvey Hill were transferred out. Only Longstreet remained with his corps.

Despite a mixed performance at Gettysburg, James Longstreet was tapped for an independent assignment away from the Army of Northern Virginia. Initially enthusiastic about the opportunity, Longstreet soon worried about his chances for success once he saw the tumultuous command situation in the Western Theater. (cm)

Lookout Mountain was the unhappy Longstreet's area of responsibility during the "siege" of Chattanooga. The lines were long and he did not have enough men to cover his sector adequately. Bragg depended on Longstreet to maintain control of Lookout Valley and Moccasin Bend. On the night of October 26–27 the Federals made their beginning moves to open what became known as the Cracker Line. William B. Hazen's brigade drifted down the Tennessee River under the noses of the Confederates on Lookout Mountain and captured Brown's Ferry, an action that Longstreet failed to report to Bragg. Longstreet seemed lethargic. Bragg was angry at Longstreet's inability to prevent the capture of Brown's Ferry and the march of Joseph Hooker's XI and XII Corps reinforcements up Lookout Valley to link up with Brown's Ferry. Longstreet ignored Bragg's order to recapture Brown's Ferry on October 27, doing nothing on that day.

On October 28, having heard no firing, a frustrated Bragg rode to the top of Lookout Mountain to confer with Longstreet. There he found Longstreet strangely lacking in initiative and uninterested in breaking up the Federal supply line. In Longstreet's opinion these new moves by the enemy were not consequential. But Bragg knew that closing this artery was crucial to Confederate success. Standing atop Lookout Mountain, both generals glassed the Federals below with their binoculars. Bragg eventually was able to get Longstreet to agree to make an attempt to interdict the Federal supply line that night.

That attempt was feeble. In what became known as the battle of Wauhatchie, Longstreet ordered some 4,000 Confederates to attack 12,000 Federals in the Valley. This night attack was a failure. The Federals maintained control of the Cracker Line, and the Confederates did nothing more to molest them. Bragg's anger at Longstreet knew no bounds, and he was more than ready to rid himself of the "overrated" James Longstreet.

By the last day in October, Bragg had determined to send Longstreet and his two divisions to operate against Ambrose E. Burnside's Federal army at Knoxville. Even though Bragg knew that Sherman's Army of the Tennessee was headed to Chattanooga to reinforce Grant and Thomas, Bragg was quick to take the gamble that Longstreet could retake Knoxville and return to Chattanooga in time to fight Grant, Thomas, Sherman, and Hooker.

Longstreet's East Tennessee Campaign is not well known to the casual Civil War student. It is into this gap that historian Ed Lowe has offered his book *A Fine Opportunity Lost* to fill the void of study between Longstreet at Chattanooga and his rejoining the Army of Northern Virginia in May 1864. Here you will learn about the importance of Knoxville to the Lincoln administration and of the large number of Union loyalists there. The battles of Campbell's Station and Fort Sanders, plus a number of other actions, are highlighted. Longstreet's challenges were many: fighting the weather, supply issues, and subordinate infighting as well as fighting Burnside's army. Maybe most importantly, Longstreet's battle with himself and his struggle with independent command would prove decisive not only to the outcome of the campaign but also to his effectiveness as a corps commander as the war continued.

ROBERT CARTER *serves as a volunteer at the Chickamauga and Chattanooga National Military Park and has authored two guidebooks on the battle of Chickamauga,* Longstreet's Breakthrough *and* Snodgrass Hill. *He has given extensive battlefield tours of both Chickamauga and Chattanooga for the last 20+ years.*

"There are many reasons for anticipating great results from the expedition against General Burnside's army with a proper force; but with the force that I now have I think it would be unreasonable to expect much. In fact, it will, in all probability, be another fine opportunity lost."

— *James Longstreet to Braxton Bragg November 11, 1863*

Prologue

Though a few months removed, the charge up Little Round Top at the battle of Gettysburg seemed distant as Col. William Oates and his men of the 15th Alabama peered into the darkness along Chattanooga's Tennessee River at Brown's Ferry. A month had passed since the Confederate victory at Chickamauga in September 1863 drove Maj. Gen. William Rosecrans's Army of the Cumberland into the confines of Chattanooga. Electing to execute a partial siege of the city and strangle Union resupply efforts, Gen. Braxton Bragg's Army of Tennessee simply sat and waited. However, one Union general drawn east chose not to wait, and that man was Maj. Gen. Ulysses S. Grant. Taking overall command in the region in mid-October, replacing Rosecrans with the "Rock of Chickamauga," Maj. Gen. George Thomas, Grant leaned upon his instinct for offensive action. A daring nighttime movement down the

A view of Lookout Mountain from Brown's Ferry landing. (el)

William Rosecrans was a roommate of Longstreet's at West Point, replaced by Maj. Gen. George Thomas in mid-October 1863. (loc)

Tennessee River on October 27, 1863, against the spread-out Confederate forces at Brown's Ferry might relieve the nagging supply issues. Awaiting to oppose this amphibious operation were the veteran soldiers of the 15th Alabama, led by Col. Oates.

Learning of a large Union force crossing the river south at Bridgeport, Alabama, Oates dispatched couriers in the late hours of October 26 to his commander, Longstreet. However, Oates did not receive any reply. With half his regiment back a few hundred yards from the river, Oates placed pickets of three to four men each 150–200 yards apart from each other. They did not wait long. Union soldiers disembarked at Brown's Ferry and scurried up the small hills surrounding the landing. For Oates, his orders were simple: place his men at one pace apart, "walk right up to the foe, and for every man to place the muzzle of his rifle against the body of a Yankee when he fired."

Overcome by sheer numbers and the penetrating darkness, it proved a fruitless maneuver. As historians Gary Laine and Morris Penny opined, "There was little the men of the 15th Alabama could do. They were surprised by a superior force and driven back."

Shouldering a toxic command climate within his army, Braxton Bragg was beside himself at the loss of Brown's Ferry. Bragg had a long-standing feud with his senior commanders, dating back to the fall of 1862. Continued disagreements prompted a visit by Confederate President Jefferson Davis to Chattanooga in early October to perhaps relieve some of Bragg's command difficulties. However, the visit by Davis failed to assuage the ill feelings Bragg and his commanders felt toward one another.

Longstreet had joined the cabal against Bragg, which only strengthened Bragg's dislike for his newest lieutenant general. A few weeks after Davis's departure, the failure at Brown's Ferry, coupled with a subsequent failure at the battle of Wauhatchie, triggered in Bragg a determination that something must be done with Longstreet.

Lurking in the shadows to the north was Maj. Gen. Ambrose Burnside's Army of the Ohio. Located in the area around Knoxville, Tennessee, Burnside offered an annoying threat to Bragg's flank. Davis wrote Bragg on October 29, proposing that he send Longstreet and his two divisions against Burnside. Bragg readily agreed and set in motion a plan to send Longstreet north, into East Tennessee to handle Burnside.

And so, Longstreet's campaign into East Tennessee commenced in early November 1863. By doing so, though, as historian Bruce Catton concluded, Bragg "had prepared the way for his own defeat."

Just three months earlier, Col. William Oates had battled for control of Little Round Top against the 20th Maine at Gettysburg. (loc)

Lookout Valley and Browns Ferry

You are now looking to the northwest

From this commanding viewpoint 1,200 feet above the river, you can see many of the historic areas associated with the Battles for Chattanooga in 1863. Among these features are Lookout Valley and Browns Ferry through which the Federals opened a vital supply line, weakening the Confederate siege of Chattanooga.

Breaking the Siege

In late September 1863, the Confederate army under Gen. Braxton Bragg laid siege to the city, trapping the Union army defeated at Chickamauga. The Confederates, positioned here on Lookout Mountain and at other key points surrounding the city, hoped to starve the Federals into submission.

At 3 a.m. on October 27, Union soldiers cast off from Chattanooga in pontoon boats and floated secretly down the river. At Browns Ferry they landed and routed the Confederate pickets. The following day they linked up with Maj. Gen. Joseph Hooker's Union forces who were moving up Lookout Valley to relieve the city. A Union supply line was thus opened, and the Confederate strangle-hold on the city was broken.

Rapid Movements
and Sudden Blows

CHAPTER ONE
SEPTEMBER 26–NOVEMBER 1, 1863

Braxton Bragg's Army of Tennessee failed to reap the benefits from the victory at Chickamauga over three days of hard fighting, September 18-20, 1863. Subordinate commanders urged a quick pursuit of the defeated enemy, but Bragg proved sluggish in his response. As a result, frustration mounted in the army's leadership.

In fact, Bragg could not shake an almost debilitating command climate in the upper echelon of his army. Less than a week after Chickamauga, lieutenant generals Leonidas Polk and James Longstreet fired off dispatches to Richmond expressing their lack of confidence in Bragg and recommending his removal. In his letter to Secretary of War James Seddon, Longstreet stated flatly, "I am convinced that nothing but the hand of God can save us or help us as long as we have our present commander."

To alleviate some of the stress, Davis reassigned Polk to Mississsippi. It did little to help. A week later, after Polk's removal from the army, Bragg's senior commanders circulated a petition amongst the ranking

The view from atop the 2,300-foot Lookout Mountain looks down on the Tennessee River toward Brown's Ferry. (el)

James Longstreet, Robert E. Lee's second in command, lobbied for attachment to the Western Theater even before Gettysburg. (loc)

officers in the army, once again requesting Bragg's removal. This statement gained a dozen signatures from corps, division, and brigade commanders and was forwarded to Richmond. No longer able to ignore what was occurring in Chattanooga, President Jefferson Davis boarded a train in early October for the city that served as the gateway to the Deep South.

On Friday, October 9, Davis arrived in Chattanooga, the stresses of the war readily apparent to all who saw him. Theodore Fogle of Company C, Second Georgia Infantry (Longstreet's Corps) observed: "He looks like the God of famine. He is a dried-up specimen of humanity."

Davis's haggard appearance did not prevent his attempt to boost army morale. He reviewed the troops, and one non-commissioned officer with the 13th Mississippi noted that they "received him with great enthusiasm and cheered vociferously as he passed along the line." Pageantry accomplished, Davis turned to the reason behind the visit: meeting with Bragg and his senior commanders.

Davis and four senior commanders in the Army of Tennessee met in Bragg's office, with the army commander sitting nervously in the corner. Davis invited Longstreet, Lt. Gen. D. H. Hill, and Maj. Gens. Simon B. Buckner and Benjamin Cheatham (who had replaced Polk) to offer their assessments of Bragg's competency. Davis went straight to Longstreet, but Longstreet tried to dodge the question, indicating he had not been with the army long enough to provide proper views. Davis pressed him until Longstreet finally expressed dissatisfaction and lack of confidence in Bragg's leadership. The other three assembled corps commanders followed Longstreet's lead.

The list of grievances failed to convince Davis, and he elected to retain Bragg in command. Davis's reason, suggested historian Steven Woodworth, "was not so much confidence in Bragg as lack of anyone better to take his place."

To relieve some of the strain within the army's high command, Davis had already moved Polk to Mississippi and now sent D. H. Hill home to North Carolina. He elevated Lt. Gen. William Hardee and Maj. Gen. John Breckinridge to corps command while sending Simon Buckner back to division command. Reflecting on those early days in October and his relationship with President Davis, Longstreet remembered, "I had no relations with him to speak of. I was not one of his favorites. In fact, I fell under his bitter displeasure for criticizing Bragg's failure to reap greater results for our Chickamauga victory."

*   *   *

Micah Jenkins represented a welcome addition to Longstreet's command in the wake of the fighting at Chickamauga. Longstreet estimated Jenkins's abilities highly, expressing his hopes for the young officer, who had graduated first in his class from the South Carolina Military Academy (now The Citadel) in 1854. Douglas Southall Freeman said Longstreet "esteemed the ambitious young South Carolinian more highly than he did any of his subordinates," save George Pickett.

Braxton Bragg assumed command of the Army of the Mississippi, later renamed the Army of Tennessee, in June 1862. (sclut)

As Braxton Bragg experienced dissension at the army level, so too did James Longstreet within his corps. Major General John Bell Hood, one of his aggressive division commanders, had received a debilitating wound on the second day of Gettysburg. Hood recovered to join Longstreet's corps at Chickamauga, but he received another wound on September 20, 1863, that required the partial amputation of his right leg. As at Gettysburg, command of the division during Hood's absence fell to another South Carolinian, Brig. Gen. Evander Law. But Longstreet preferred Jenkins. While Davis was in Chattanooga, Longstreet asked the president to promote Jenkins to major general and assign him permanent command of the division. Davis refused the request. Davis also refused to promote Evander Law to major general. When Davis departed without a decision on who might command Hood's division permanently, he "allowed that controversy to fester." By default, Jenkins retained command as Longstreet's preferred choice. Moreover, Jenkins's date of rank made him the logical option over Law.

Before returning to Richmond, Davis praised the men of the Army of Tennessee for their victory at Chickamauga. In his remarks, he also offered a thinly veiled admonition on the importance of cooperation within the army. "To zeal you have added gallantry; to gallantry, energy; to energy, fortitude," he congratulated the men. But, he said, the troops must "crown these with harmony, due subordination, and cheerful support to lawful authority, that the measure of your duty may be full."

And with that, Davis left Bragg to regain control of the army with the hopes his commanders might fall into line.

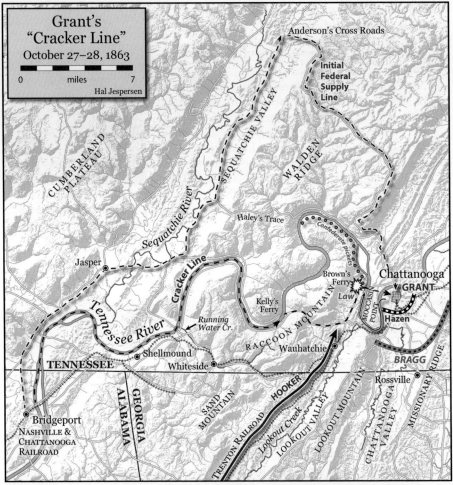

GRANT'S "CRACKER LINE"—Operational picture of Chattanooga in October 1863. The attack on Brown's Ferry, October 27, 1863, helped open the Union supply line into Chattanooga.

One Confederate soldier, observing the chaos that seemed ubiquitous across Bragg's command, concluded, "[t]his is a mess very different from anything we ever had under Lee." The soldier's remarks augured poorly for Bragg. An army in the best of shape might have struggled with the challenge that confronted the North Carolinian and his men: defeating Maj. Gen. Ulysses S. Grant, now overseeing Union operations in Chattanooga. Davis's indifference to the trials of Bragg's command left his army in something much less than the best of shape.

Grant's successful Brown's Ferry operation soon insured the flow of Federal supplies into Chattanooga. With growing unease, Longstreet and Bragg watched from atop Lookout Mountain in late October as U.S.

forces built up their strength around the ferry. Bragg was justifiably angered as events unfolded. Longstreet never fully appreciated the military value of the valley to the west, which would soon serve as an entryway for Federal supplies.

In response, Longstreet hatched a plan to attack U.S. forces at Wauhatchie, a few miles south of Brown's Ferry. Undertaken as a night operation on October 29, 1863, the attack failed—and recriminations and accusations flowed across Jenkins's division. "I can only attribute the want of conduct," Longstreet stated in his official report, "among the brigadier generals."

Perhaps strengthening the jealousy between Jenkins and Law, Longstreet placed the blame not on Col. John Bratton, who led the main assault against U.S. forces, "but rather on Law's inability to hold off Hooker's reinforcing column." Longstreet also cast blame on Brig. Gen. Jerome Robertson, leading the Texas Brigade, relieving him of command for a want of cooperation during the night action. However, Bragg would overrule Longstreet in the Robertson case and restore him to command shortly after Longstreet began his march to Knoxville.

The march would come as the result of a suggestion from Davis on October 29. Why not send Longstreet north to operate against Ambrose Burnside, the president asked. Bragg—almost incredulous over the loss of Brown's Ferry and then the botched action at Wauhatchie—readily concurred.

Ulysses S. Grant commanded the newly formed Military Division of the Mississippi, which included the armies of the Cumberland, Ohio, and Tennessee. (loc)

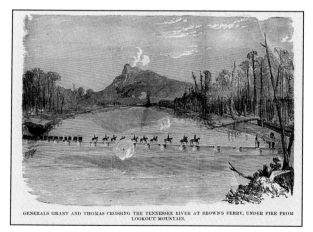

GENERALS GRANT AND THOMAS CROSSING THE TENNESSEE RIVER AT BROWN'S FERRY, UNDER FIRE FROM LOOKOUT MOUNTAIN.

With the capture of Brown's Ferry, Grant could now get much-needed supplies flowing into Chattanooga. This greatly upset Bragg's attempt to starve the Union army. (hw)

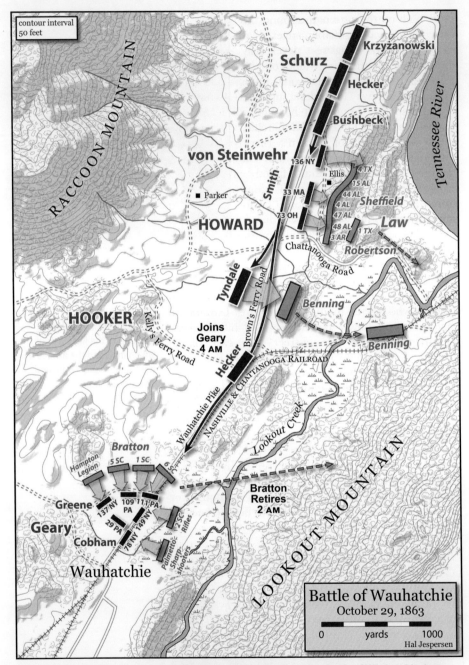

BATTLE OF WAUHATCHIE—The failed Confederate night operation at the battle of Wauhatchie, just three miles south of Brown's Ferry on October 29, 1863. A steady defense by Union general John Geary held off Confederate assaults during the early morning hours.

By dispatching Longstreet to Knoxville, the Army of Tennessee commander might reopen the rail line that ran through Knoxville and thereby regain communications to Richmond through East Tennessee. Additionally, having Longstreet on Grant's flank might force Grant to relinquish Chattanooga altogether, perhaps even allowing Bragg to gain control of Middle Tennessee (which he had lost during the preceding year's disastrous Tullahoma Campaign). Maybe, in Davis's thinking, doing anything in a proactive, forward action was better than simply sitting idly by, waiting for U.S. forces to build in greater strength. Unfortunately in this instance, as Bragg executed Davis's suggestion to send Longstreet away, the decision "carried out was worse than no action at all."

Bragg saw clear evidence of U.S. forces gaining strength almost daily in Chattanooga, and he knew Maj. Gen. William Sherman's men would soon arrive in full force, yet he still decided to dispatch Longstreet's two divisions northward. "Bragg wasted no time in sending Longstreet on his way," noted historian Donald Stoker, "and Longstreet wasted no time going."

It would be hard going for Longstreet's men. There was probably no worse-equipped force in Bragg's army than Longstreet's men. They had departed Virginia greatly deficient in wagons, horses, mules, and personal baggage—a fact that had repercussions once cold weather arrived in East Tennessee.

In his memoirs, Grant observed that sending Longstreet away was not a sound tactical or operational decision. Grant judged Bragg harshly for "reducing his own force more than one-third and depriving himself of the presence of the ablest general of his command." Stanley Horn, an early historian of the Army of Tennessee, wondered whether "a seasoned soldier like Bragg [could] fail to realize the folly of dividing his forces in the face of an ever-strong enemy?" Horn then queried: "Was he willing to do almost anything to get rid of Longstreet?" Apparently, the answer was yes.

Longstreet's force "made about fifteen thousand men, after deducting camp guards and foraging parties." He had, of course, the two divisions that came down from Virginia, McLaws's and Hood's, the latter now commanded by Micah Jenkins. McLaws had the experienced brigades of Brig. Gens. Joseph B. Kershaw, Benjamin G. Humphreys, William Wofford,

Micah Jenkins graduated first in his class from the South Carolina Military Academy, now The Citadel, in 1854. (loc)

and Goode Bryan. Jenkins, as acting division commander, led the battle-hardened brigades of Brig. Gens. George T. Anderson, Henry L. Benning, Evander M. Law, and Jerome Robertson. Longstreet counted on the dependable Lt. Col. Edward Porter Alexander (promoted to brigadier general in February 1864) and Maj. Austin Leyden to oversee his artillery. Bragg also deployed cavalry to support Longstreet, led by Maj. Gen. Joseph Wheeler. Wheeler organized his cavalry into two divisions, one under Maj. Gen. W. T. Martin and the other under Brig. Gen. Frank Armstrong.

The notion that Longstreet's departure constituted an independent command for Lee's "Old Warhorse" is pure fiction. Bragg made clear that Longstreet should run Burnside out of East Tennessee and capture or destroy him. Bragg urged Longstreet to depend strongly "on rapid movements and sudden blows." Keeping communications open between Longstreet and Chattanooga was also essential, "as it may become necessary in an emergency to recall you temporarily," Bragg explained.

A few weeks before Longstreet moved north, Bragg had sent the division of Maj. Gen. Carter Stevenson to keep a watchful eye on Burnside, followed later by Brig. Gen. John K. Jackson's division. Longstreet felt linking up with Stevenson might prove advantageous in executing Bragg's directives, especially if he could do so quickly and efficiently. But he had no explicit orders to do so.

The best-laid plans of Bragg and Longstreet soon encountered snags. As Porter Alexander explained in *Military Memoirs of a Confederate*, Longstreet planned a move via train from Chattanooga's Tyner Station to Sweetwater, Tennessee. He hoped to arrive in Sweetwater, some forty miles from Knoxville, by November 7–8. However, as Longstreet's units converged on their departure points, they soon encountered a frustratingly inadequate transportation system. This proved only a harbinger of things to come for Longstreet and his veterans.

Troubling for Longstreet, Grant could not fail to realize the importance of East Tennessee. President Lincoln reminded without end his competent and resourceful commander, "Remember Burnside." Lincoln held a strong affinity for the region of Tennessee Burnside occupied. Keep that in mind when shaping future operations, Lincoln told him. Having at long last occupied East Tennessee, bringing

a measure of relief to the loyal occupants, Lincoln wanted to be sure Grant understood that this vital territory was not to be given up.

New York monument commemorating the battle of Wauhatchie. (el)

"For the Noble People of East Tennessee"

CHAPTER TWO
OCTOBER 23–NOVEMBER 1, 1863

The Henegar house in Charleston, Tennessee, served as a headquarters for both Confederate and U.S. generals, including Union Gen. William T. Sherman. According to family tradition, on the porch of the home, Sherman advised Mrs. Henegar to leave the South, which she replied she would not. Sherman warned her that when he was finished, not even a bird would live there. (el)

East Tennessee was of vital logistical and operational importance for both the U.S. and the Confederacy. The area provided an ample supply of corn and wheat to a healthy stock of horses and mules. In addition, two railroads in East Tennessee provided vital transportation capability. The East Tennessee and Georgia railroad ran from Knoxville to Cleveland, Tennessee, where the track split, with one branch proceeding on to Chattanooga and the other to Dalton, Georgia. The East Tennessee and Virginia Railroad started in Bristol, Virginia. The railroad concluded its journey in Knoxville. The Confederacy relied on this railroad to maintain effective communications from Virginia to the Western theater of operations. Commanders also relied on a navigable river, the Tennessee, and a macadamized turnpike for the transportation of resources.

The area also contained important mineral resources for fighting a war. Southwestern Virginia had an ample supply of salt and lead, while southeastern Tennessee had copper.

Since his election in 1861, President Abraham Lincoln always kept a keen eye toward the loyalists in East Tennessee. (loc)

East Tennessee also possessed strong Union sentiment. During the secession crisis, the Lincoln administration sought to leverage this support to keep Tennessee in the Union. Although the effort failed, Lincoln considered the region to be of primary strategic importance throughout the war. He hoped to gain and maintain access to eastern Tennessee, eventually liberating the region.

High mountain regions to the east and west, and the valleys in East Tennessee, limited the local population from providing sustainable markets across the region. Consequently, Knoxville became the hub of this valley, at least in the early days of its settlement. Moreover, with a large hog- and corn-based economy, the ownership of slaves in the region was not as widespread as in other parts of the state. However, the appearance of railroads expanded market farming. Wheat production, for example, expanded more than 300 percent from 1850 to 1860. With this growth came an expansion of slavery—21 percent for that same period.

Despite Confederate efforts to hold onto East Tennessee, the area remained remarkably pro-Union. During the balloting for secession in late 1861, East Tennesseans voted 2 to 1 to remain in the Union. Voter intimidation and Confederate soldiers casting illegal ballots undoubtedly made these results even closer than actual public sentiment. Northerners came to identify with the defiant East Tennesseans, a display that encouraged the Lincoln administration to pay close attention to the non-secessionist region. Like the country it abandoned, East Tennessee was divided and struggling to find its own identity. Historian Aaron Astor noted East Tennessee was "being pulled in directions it did not want to go" and "pulled into a war it did not seek."

Lincoln emphasized the importance of holding onto Chattanooga in particular, and he felt assured "the rebellion must dwindle and die" if his commanders embraced the same commitment. The president demonstrated that commitment by moving supplies into the region, assigning Grant to Chattanooga, and dispatching two corps from George Meade's Army of the Potomac. He also repositioned the bulk of Sherman's corps from Mississippi to Chattanooga.

William Sherman replaced Grant as commander of the Army of the Tennessee after President Lincoln reorganized U.S. forces in the west. (loc)

"The safety of Burnside's army and the loyal people of East Tennessee had been the subject of much anxiety to the president for several months, during which time he was doing all he could do to relieve the situation," Grant wrote in his memoirs.

President Abraham Lincoln removed Ambrose Burnside from command of the Army of the Potomac after the army's December 1862 loss at Fredericksburg. Burnside is depicted here entering Knoxville in September 1863.

(mhc)

One historian has noted that, for the loyal Union population, the president was "ever alive with the keenest sympathy for the noble people of East Tennessee." In a reply to a letter from two concerned residents of that region, Lincoln wrote, "You do not estimate the holding of East Tennessee more highly than I do."

While the transfer of troops and leadership into the area mirrored an increased emphasis on this region, the residents of East Tennessee understood they had no better friend than Ambrose Burnside. Having occupied Knoxville in early September 1863 as something of a conquering hero, Burnside showed a commitment to the pro-Unionist population and a strong intent to hold on to the captured territory. The citizens of East Tennessee had positive feelings toward Burnside and knew he was not going to abandon them.

Burnside faced a mighty task. U.S. Secretary of War Edwin Stanton had dispatched his assistant, Charles Dana, to the Army of the Cumberland prior to the battle of Chickamauga. In early November, Dana

proceeded to Knoxville to discuss operations with
Burnside. Dana reported that Burnside had roughly
thirty-three thousand men, yet the units of the Army
of the Ohio "were scattered all the way from Kentucky,
by Cumberland Gap, down to Knoxville. In and
about Knoxville he had not concentrated more than
twelve thousand to fourteen thousand men." Burnside
had a vast territory to cover, his forces stretched thin.
Dana concluded that Burnside could not "resist an
attack by a large force." Dana also detected a lack of
experienced combat leaders within the army's four
small divisions, each equally distributed across the IX
and XXIII Corps. Dana referred to this deficiency as
a "great want of first-rate general officers, both the 9th
and 23rd Corps being commanded by brigadiers who
are comparatively inexperienced."

Adding to his issues, Burnside had battled an
intestinal problem since October. He petitioned for
some rest and "relief from his constant and harassing
duties." Burnside even submitted his resignation
as operations around Chattanooga heated up. The
president declined his offer, stating, "A thousand
thanks for the late successes you have given us. We
cannot allow you to resign, until things shall be a
little more settled in East Tennessee." Burnside went
back to work around Knoxville upon receiving the
president's response. Even in ill health, Burnside was

still physically imposing. Charles Dana found a man of impressive stature, over six feet in height, "an energetic, decided man, frankly, manly, and well educated."

Looking northward, Longstreet recognized the challenge that confronted him as he left Chattanooga. Shelby Foote observed a precarious situation in Chattanooga upon Longstreet's departure. The town was "dangerously exposed to an assault by Grant, who already had been reinforced by Hooker and presumably would soon be joined as well by the even larger force marching eastward under Sherman." Bragg needed Longstreet to handle affairs in East Tennessee quickly before Grant could take the offensive. Grant had already demonstrated in past campaigns an ability to muster forces in short order.

Such a concentration might also include Burnside's forces. Carter Stevenson's Confederate division kept a watchful eye on Burnside should he move toward Chattanooga and a junction with Grant.

Longstreet prepared to venture north in the hopes of a fast, decisive engagement, counting on the Confederate transportation system for movement north. Unfortunately, the system was overburdened by military demands for which it had never been constructed. Any hope Bragg or Longstreet held for a speedy dispatch of Burnside quickly became an impossibility. Frustration soon arose among Longstreet's command instead.

LONGSTREET'S CROSSING

1E 76

Lt. Gen. James Longstreet, C.S.A., in his drive for Knoxville crossed the Tennessee River at Huff's Ferry a half mile to the north on a pontoon bridge, Nov. 13-15, 1863. He thus eluded a Federal force across the river on the east side of Loudon.

TENNESSEE HISTORICAL COMMISSION

More Against Longstreet than Burnside

CHAPTER THREE
NOVEMBER 2–NOVEMBER 15, 1863

The approximate Confederate crossing point at Huff's Ferry, just outside of Loudon, Tennessee. Longstreet's forces crossed here beginning in the late hours of November 13, 1863. (el)

In any military operation, accurate intelligence about avenues of approach, key terrain features, and potential obstacles can determine success or failure. In the Civil War, the tools available to a commander to gather such intelligence included cavalry forces deployed out front (which Longstreet had); local civilians (difficult in a pro-Union area); or maps of the region (which Longstreet had in limited number).

Before departure, Longstreet submitted a request for maps. He also requested the assignment of officers to the commissary and anyone familiar with the resources available in the region. He even requested an engineering officer to accompany him, someone who had served under Maj. Gen. Simon Buckner when Buckner had operated in the Knoxville area. Other than a topographical map of the country between the Hiawassee and Little Tennessee rivers, these requests went unfilled.

Sensing a need, and at Longstreet's request, Buckner provided intelligence on the network of roads and streams between Loudon and Knoxville.

Moving into an area of operations almost devoid of such intelligence could prove hazardous to Longstreet's force. However, Buckner had to provide his information from afar. Subsequent to Davis's visit to Chattanooga in early October, Bragg had stripped Buckner of his department and corps-level command, relegating him to division command. Not long thereafterward, Buckner took a medical leave of absence to Virginia as a way to remove himself from Bragg's command. The lack of boots-on-the-ground insight would hamper Longstreet and, unfortunately, other problems confronted him as well.

In the same message Bragg had sent to Longstreet expecting "rapid movements and sudden blows," the army commander assured Longstreet that "every preparation is ordered to advance you as fast as possible." This promise failed to match conditions on the ground. "We were so dependent on Bragg's vision, which cruelly failed us," said Longstreet's staff officer, Moxley Sorrel. "Not to dwell too long on these mishaps, I need only add that they beset the entire campaign."

Longstreet and his team anticipated Bragg's quartermaster would have trains available once the soldiers assembled at Tyner's Station outside of Chattanooga. However, the trains were not ready until November 5. Even then, said Sorrel, the trains

In November 1863, the Sweetwater Depot was the northernmost station held by the Confederacy as they advanced against Knoxville. (el)

were "almost comical in their inefficiency." When going up steep grades, the locomotives were so poor that the soldiers had to disembark and march up to the summit before reboarding.

Some of the brigades had to make their way to Sweetwater entirely on foot. Commanders directed soldiers along the way to "find the cars where they might have the good fortune to meet them." Consequently the brigades arrived slowly, over several days.

Longstreet preceded the main body to Sweetwater, expecting to find all the supplies required to sustain his command. Incensed at the lack of logistical support, Longstreet penned a note to Lt. Col. George Brent, a member of Bragg's staff. Without such support, "I suppose that we shall not be able to make any movements," Longstreet stated bluntly, continuing, "I doubt whether we can more than subsist in the country, doing nothing else, with our present limited and inefficient transportation."

Constructed in 1854, the Niota Depot is the only Civil War-era depot that currently sits along the East Tennessee and Georgia Railroad line. (el)

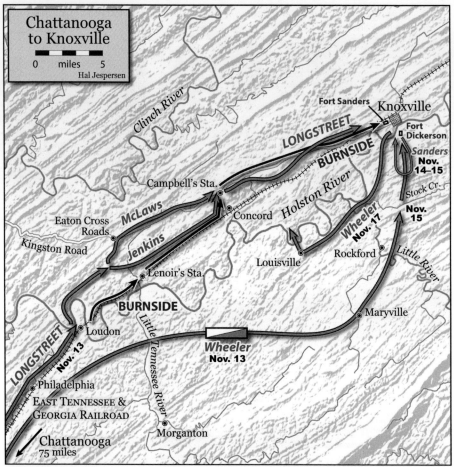

CHATTANOOGA TO KNOXVILLE—An inefficient rail system made transportation of Longstreet's command toward Knoxville a frustrating journey. A failed opportunity at Campbell's Station raised further doubt among Longstreet's officers about the East Tennesse campaign.

Even Maj. Raphael Moses, Longstreet's commissary chief, could not ignore the dire situation facing the soldiers upon arrival in Sweetwater. Moses observed the department was "utterly unprovided for, and its condition as bad as it could be in a country not utterly exhausted." One Confederate soldier complained about wagons breaking down constantly, worn-out saddles and harnesses for the horses, and other problems. The supply situation was "beyond all question the worst I ever saw."

To Longstreet's astonishment, Maj. Gen. Carter Stevenson soon informed him that Bragg had directed Stevenson to ship all supplies to the main army in Chattanooga. Taking in the misery that made up the supply and transportation system in the early stages of this campaign, Longstreet uttered after the war, "It began to look more like a campaign against Longstreet than against Burnside."

Bragg reminded Longstreet to hasten his movements against Burnside; time was of the essence. As Longstreet biographer Jeffry Wert noted, "The army commander blamed Longstreet . . . for not utilizing his authority and taking the wagons that were along the road."

Longstreet would have none of it. "There are many reasons for anticipating great results from the expedition against General Burnside's army with a proper force," Longstreet wrote to Bragg on November 11, "but with the force I now have I think it would be unreasonable to expect much. In fact, it will, in all probability, be another fine opportunity lost."

Consistent with this tense relationship, the next day Bragg responded to Longstreet: "Your several dispatches of today astonish me. . . . The means being furnished, you were expected to handle your own troops, and I cannot understand your constant applications for me to furnish them."

Longstreet retorted: "You are very much mistaken in supposing that any authority over transportation has ever been extended to me. I have several times made known to you our delays, and your dispatch just received is the first intimation that I could exercise any authority."

Writing his memoirs after the war, Longstreet concluded, "His effort to make his paper record at my expense was not pleasing, but I tried to endure it with patience. He knew that trains and conductors were under his exclusive control, but he wanted papers that would throw the responsibility of delay to another's shoulders."

The bulk of Longstreet's troops assembled around the Sweetwater area on November 12, meaning the next phase of the operation could finally commence. However, the lack of wagons for hauling the pontoon bridges further disrupted his plans. Longstreet had originally hoped to move around Knoxville, to the rear of the city through Morganton and Maryville, flanking Burnside. Moving forward along the south bank, though, would require three major river crossings: the Little Tennessee River, the Little River, and the Holston River. Given the lack of animals to carry the required crossing material and no rail line running near the south bank, Longstreet was left with few options. "[T]he only practical route was to go

Edward Porter Alexander served as Lt. Gen. James Longstreet's artillery chief for the East Tennessee Campaign. He helped select the crossing site at Huff's Ferry in Loudon, Tennessee. He grew frustrated with his lack of involvement in the attack at Fort Sanders and missed an opportunity to damage U.S. forces at Bean's Station. (loc)

Albert S. Lenoir was a respected engineer and surveyor. In 1839, Lenoir visited Ross's Landing and laid out what was to become the city of Chattanooga. This was the home he built upon his return back to Loudon County. (el)

where the East Tennessee and Georgia Railroad could deliver the bridge," one historian later noted.

This meant crossing to the north bank of the Tennessee River at Loudon, some thirty miles downriver from Knoxville and on the same side of the river, "and to make direct march upon Knoxville by that route," Longstreet recalled after the war. Longstreet directed Porter Alexander, and Maj. John J. Clarke, his chief engineer, to reconnoiter a crossing point in the Loudon area.

Loudon lay northeast of Sweetwater, on the south bank of the Tennessee River, which flows mostly westward. Lenoir, or Lenoir's Station, lay further east, just upstream and on the north bank of the river, opposite where the Little Tennessee River commenced. Longstreet mistakenly thought this was the French Broad River—an error that would come into play later in Knoxville. The topography and, more importantly, Longstreet's imperfect understanding of the land and river networks, hindered his operations throughout the campaign.

The Confederates had destroyed the Loudon railroad bridge in early September after their withdrawal from Knoxville, so Longstreet had to choose another crossing site. Longstreet's staff selected Huff's Ferry as the best place to build up the pontoon bridge. Though only three-quarters of a mile from the railroad located in Loudon, the twisting pattern of the river at that point made the crossing six miles by road.

The current at the pontoon bridge's location was quite strong and, with inadequate anchors, the bridge slowly began to sway back and forth. The bridge eventually settled into a unique letter-S shape in the river—though, as one Confederate soldier

The railroad at Loudon, Tennessee, changed hands a number of times during the war. The bridge was strategically critical for traffic between Richmond and Chattanooga. The Confederacy depended on the railroad to transport troops, salt, and lead from Southwest Virginia, as well as copper and food from East Tennessee. (ol)

LOUDON RAILROAD BRIDGE
★ ★ ★
Strategic Crossing

The covered wooden bridge of the East Tennessee and Georgia Railroad here on the Tennessee River was a strategically significant crossing for the railroad between Richmond and Chattanooga.

100 cars. In December, as Union Gen. William T. Sherman's army approached Knoxville, the Confederates ran the train equipment into the river, abandoning the bridge site to the Federals.

The Union army controlled the site for the remainder of the war. Engineers completed a temporary bridge by April 1864 and a more permanent bridge by November. In February 1865, Arthur D. Wharton and

This defensive position in Loudon contained one of the Confederate redans (earthworks for cannons and troops with an opening to the rear) that protected the Loudon Railroad Bridge. Both Confederate and U.S. troops built camps and huts along this area of the Tennessee River. (el)

remembered, "no man should abuse the bridge by which he safely crosses, and this one took us over, using care and caution."

On November 13, Longstreet's cavalry commander, Maj. Gen. Joseph Wheeler, left five Georgia regiments at Sweetwater and then, under Longstreet's direction, sent the bulk of his horse soldiers to ford the Little Tennessee River and seize the heights south of Knoxville—a task Longstreet originally intended for his main body of infantry. Longstreet, meanwhile, crossed his main force at Loudon on November 14.

*   *   *

Burnside and Grant now faced the challenge of developing a strategy that mitigated any threat Longstreet might pose to either of their forces.

Despite ever-increasing manpower, Grant remained hesitant to strike at Bragg's defenses in Chattanooga. Yet Grant had cause for concern about Burnside's position, fearing a lack of transportation assets should he have to withdraw from East

Tennessee—something authorities in Washington would not condone, anyway. To mitigate the pressure, Grant directed the new commander of the Army of the Cumberland, Maj. Gen. George Thomas, to make some type of demonstration against Bragg on November 7. Thomas, though, expressed operational and logistical concerns, and Grant backed off in frustration. He would have to wait for Sherman to arrive with his entire force before making his next move.

Meanwhile, Burnside traveled down from Knoxville to assume command of operations around the Loudon area.

As Longstreet was in full river-crossing operations, Grant reminded Burnside on November 14 "it is of the most vital importance that East Tennessee should be held. Take immediate steps to that end." Burnside recognized the threat—but also the opportunity. Whatever damage the battle of Fredericksburg had inflicted on Burnside's reputation, his performance and operational strategy in East Tennessee, particularly in November 1863, deserves praise.

In late November 1863, William Sherman led the Union relief force through Philadelphia toward Morganton and the Little Tennessee River. The corps arrived at the Morganton Crossing, which is now under water. The troops constructed a bridge on December 4 and commenced crossing operations. (el)

Delaying briefly Longstreet's crossing at the Tennessee River was an option. However, Burnside elected a different strategy. Gathering his headquarters staff, now in the Loudon area, Burnside indicated he was going to withdraw the command to Knoxville. His staff countered they could defend along the river, throwing the Confederates back across.

Burnside understood this, as he mentioned in his official report: "Knowing the purposes of General Grant as I did, I decided that he could be better served by driving Longstreet farther away from Bragg than by checking him at the river, and I accordingly decided to withdraw my forces and retreat leisurely toward Knoxville, and soon after daylight on the 15th the whole command was on the road."

Therefore, while Bragg directed Longstreet to complete his mission quickly and return to Chattanooga, Longstreet would now have to chase Burnside's Army of the Ohio all the way to Knoxville to complete that task. Grant approved Burnside's plan and envisioned Longstreet stuck in the middle between two U.S. forces, Grant and Burnside.

The National Campground in Greenback, Tennessee, is listed on the National Register of Historic Places. The Tabernacle Shed was constructed in 1874, from timber donated by local farmers. It was designed to reconcile the differences between opposing sides of the Civil War, "to allay the feuds engendered by the late national difficulties," according to the campground records. To this day, services are held every September for five evenings. (el)

In the early morning hours of November 16, Burnside slowly pulled away from Lenoir's Station. Colonel William Humphrey's brigade of the IX Corps served as Burnside's rearguard, with the 17th Michigan being the last unit in line.

Burnside issued Field Order No. 81 directing the XXIII Corps to destroy their wagons, ammunition trains, camp furniture, and officers' baggage at Lenoir's Station. The men were to use their animals to pull the artillery and its ammunition. Because heavy rains had turned many of the roads in the area to mud, in some instances twenty to twenty-four animals were used for each artillery piece, making travel extremely difficult. "About one hundred wagons, heavily loaded with army supplies, were abandoned because we had not time to burn them," one soldier from the 17th Michigan observed. "A large amount of bread, bacon, sugar, and clothing were thus turned over to Longstreet's quartermaster."

Longstreet's ordnance officer, Maj. Francis W. Dawson, discovered over 170,000 rounds of small arms ammunition, of which 100,000 remained serviceable. Dawson observed between four to five inches of usable gunpowder scattered all across the ground. The soldiers took it upon themselves to strike a match to their pipe and enjoy the abundance of powder around them, "and several of my men indulged themselves in that way to my great discomfort."

Brushing aside the shy resistance at the Tennessee River and accumulating what he could from supplies left behind, Longstreet analyzed what limited intelligence he had to determine his best feasible course of action. The route to Knoxville offered only a few options, and Longstreet set his sights on a crossroads not far from his current location, Campbell's Station. While operations had not developed at the pace and efficiency he would have liked, Longstreet saw an opportunity at this crossroads. Finally, perhaps, there could be a decisive battle.

The Battle of Campbell's Station

CHAPTER FOUR
NOVEMBER 16, 1863

The incessant rain and East Tennessee red clay left a lasting impression on Confederate and Union soldiers alike. One U.S. soldier noted the clay was neither as slippery as soap nor sticky as wax, but that it was nonetheless a serious impediment to any forward movement: "in less urgent circumstances the roads would have been considered almost impassable."

But passable it had to be for both Burnside and Longstreet, the former in withdrawal and the latter in pursuit.

Burnside set his withdrawal from Lenoir's Station in the late hours of November 15 and into the early hours of November 16. Colonel John F. Hartranft's Second Division of the IX Corps moved along the Lenoir Road to secure the vital intersection around Campbell's Station. With solid reasoning, Burnside feared that if Longstreet captured the intersection, it could very well cut off the Federal army's march to Knoxville.

The roads being what they were made the task all the more difficult. One soldier of the 35th Massachusetts Infantry helped support the movement

During the battle of Campbell's Station, the U.S. and Confederate soldiers used the Campbell's Station Inn to shelter the wounded. Blood stains can still be seen on the pine floors. (el)

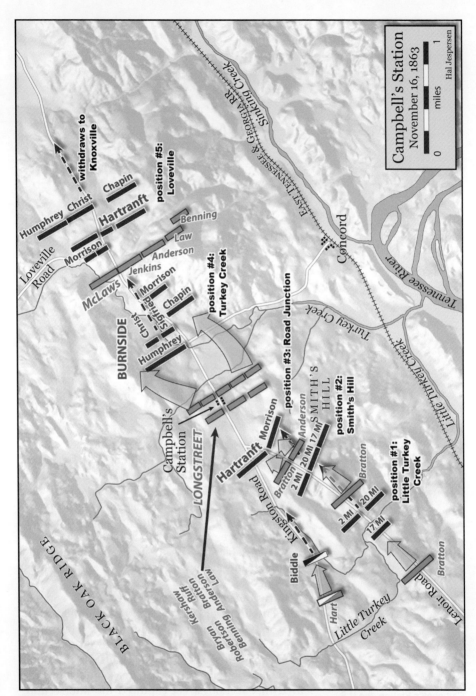

CAMPBELL'S STATION—The race to the intersection proved critical, allowing Burnside time to organize a defense. Miscommunications delayed Longstreet's attack. Burnside gradually withdrew, luring Longstreet closer to Knoxville and further away from Chattanooga.

of the artillery batteries, a frustratingly arduous mission. With the horses nearly exhausted, "the men caught hold of the muddy rims of wheels or parts of gun carriages, wherever a hand could seize them and pushed and shoved to assist the animals." The soldier recalled it took nearly eight hours to move just three miles. Another soldier from the 51st Pennsylvania Infantry described it as almost an accordion effect. Both men and horses struggled to release one cannon from the thick mud and, once secured on solid ground, they would go back and pull another forward, "so on until the bottomless mire was wrought through."

Muddy roads aside, Burnside had to be careful. The East Tennessee and Georgia Railroad went from Lenoir's Station to Knoxville, crossing the vital Old Kingston Road just west of the city. Burnside could not follow the railroad directly because the twisting Tennessee River lay immediately to his right, provoking a realistic fear of having his army trapped between the Old Kingston Road and the river. Beating Longstreet to Campbell's Station was Burnside's only choice to continue his withdrawal toward Knoxville in safety.

Longstreet moved his force in two columns. His 42-year-old division commander, Maj. Gen. Lafayette McLaws, went north along the Kingston Road to Eaton Crossroads, advancing toward Campbell's Station from the north. Meanwhile, Longstreet accompanied the division of Brig. Gen. Micah Jenkins along the southernmost approach to the crossroads, following the withdrawing elements of Burnside's army. For artillery support, Alexander divided his guns between the two advancing columns. If all went according to plan, Jenkins would drive Burnside into the expecting arms of McLaws's division as it waited to receive the withdrawing U.S. forces at Campbell's Station. Yet, like their U.S. counterparts, the "lightly-clad Confederate soldiers" found that the repeated rains and plunging temperatures made for rough going.

One advantage Longstreet did have over Burnside was that his supply wagons and trains could lag behind the infantry and artillery columns as they advanced. Burnside could not afford such a luxury. After destroying what he could back at Lenoir's Station, Burnside had to push everything else forward—the fighting as well as the supporting elements—lest they get captured by the approaching Confederate forces.

With the weather causing difficulties for both forces, Burnside had few courses of action that

Colonel John F. Hartranft (above) led a division in the IX Corps. Hartranft barely beat the division of Lafayette McLaws to the critical crossroads at Campbell's Station. Hartranft is also known for serving as the commanding officer at the Old Capitol Prison in Washington, D.C. and special provost marshal during the trial of the Lincoln conspirators. When asked if they had any final statements before their death, George Atzerodt and Lewis Paine spoke highly of the treatment from Hartranft and his men. Following the prayers, Hartranft read the order of the War Department, carrying out the President's executive order for the execution (right). (loc)

would allow him to withdraw his army safely from the trap Longstreet expected to spring. Longstreet hoped the coming fight might prove more fruitful than past battles, generating something significant for the Confederate cause. It all hinged on the exactness of purpose and synchronization of forces across his command, something elusive in past efforts.

Major Byron Cutcheon of the 20th Michigan commented in his official report that "no actual collision occurred until we reached a point about a mile from the junction of the Kingston with the [Lenoir] Road. Here a stand was made."

A skillfully planned delaying action by Burnside bore its fruits during the battle of Campbell's Station. "Hartranft, after securing all the roads, sent a force of about 200 mounted men of Biddle's along the Kingston Road with orders to move forward till they found the enemy and then attack," wrote Brig. Gen. Robert Potter of the IX Corps. A fighting withdrawal occurred as they moved east along the Kingston Road. Subsequently, Colonel Hartranft's command—a mixture of infantry and cavalry—formed his two brigades in line of battle north of the Kingston Road. Units from Brig. Gen. Edward Ferrero's division began to occupy ground to Hartranft's left flank. By now, Jenkins's division was pressing heavily on the Lenoir Road, with the division of McLaws attacking along the Kingston Road. By some estimates, the U.S. forces arrived just minutes ahead of McLaws's, whose lead regiments found their way just west of Campbell's Station, blocked by Burnside's ever-increasing force at the road junction."

The IX Corps troops formed a second line of defense just past the Nelson-Russell home, while wagons and artillery moved past the home to secure new positions. Meanwhile, Col. William Humphrey had the honor to serve as the rear guard. "I commenced moving my line to the rear," Humphrey wrote after the battle, "halting at every few rods, facing about, and checking the enemy, who was now crowding on in strong force." Humphrey, too, fell back to the new position, executing a series of leap-frog engagements to delay the Confederate movements.

Further to the east, Burnside spread his forces across a valley between two low hills, roughly a mile apart. With McLaws on the left and Jenkins's division coming up on the right, Longstreet intended to have one of McLaws's brigades and a cavalry brigade create a diversion against Burnside's right flank. Longstreet directed that Jenkins send two of his brigades "through a well-covered way off our right to march out well past the enemy's left and strike against that flank and rear." Yet, Longstreet already provided a disclaimer before giving battle, stating "our severe travel and labor after leaving Virginia were not to find an opportunity to make a simply successful battle."

With forces finally assembled, the battle of Campbell's Station took shape.

*   *   *

On November 16, Longstreet finally had his two divisions consolidated and ready to attack. Lafayette McLaws moved his division down the Kingston Road.

Dr. William Nelson owned this home at the time of the battle. During the battle of Campbell's Station, Dr. Nelson attended to the wounded, both U.S. and Confederate soldiers. (el)

Meanwhile, Micah Jenkins deployed his division to the right of McLaws's division. Longstreet ordered Jenkins's brigades to peel away, off to the south of the Kingston Road, and form a line of battle. Evander Law's brigade was to move out beyond the Federal left, eastward until they were on the flank or to the rear of Hartranft's left flank.

Confusion among the division commanders over who was to launch the attack cost precious time. Jenkins lost his patience and galloped off to see Longstreet, questioning what the delay was. Finally, around 3:00 p.m. Longstreet started Anderson's and Law's brigades around the Federal left. As the senior ranking officer, Law assumed command of the flanking movement.

Daylight soon faded, though, and unfortunately for Longstreet's men, visibility greatly diminished. After Law and Anderson moved toward the Federal left, Jenkins "received a message from General Law that in advancing, his brigade had obliqued so much to the left as to have gotten out of its line of attack." With Anderson and Law's brigades now practically in front of the Federal lines, Jenkins called off Anderson's attack and told Law to press on. However, once darkness settled in, a second attempt to strike the left flank proved impracticable. Jenkins concluded that Law's "causeless and inexcusable movement lost us the few moments in which success from this point could be attained." The animus between the two commanders, growing since the previous month, now seemed to strengthen with every action.

A skillful series of maneuvers to the rear by Burnside accomplished the goal of pulling Longstreet away from Chattanooga. Brigadier General Julius White of the XXIII Corps commented in his official report that, as soldiers moved, they "frequently halt[ed] and fac[ed] about to the enemy, not a man hurrying his step or otherwise disfiguring the movement, although subjected to severe fire from the enemy's artillery, which had been rapidly advanced to short range."

Longstreet lamented that Burnside's withdrawal—and the Confederate failure to pursue him—resulted in a lost opportunity. Still, long after the fighting concluded, Old Pete could only agree that Burnside's "retreat was very cleverly conducted."

Had Longstreet been victorious, the Confederates could have recovered "East Tennessee, and in all probability captured the greater portion of the enemy's forces," Longstreet later mused. It was not to

Evander M. Law was a fellow South Carolinian along with Micah Jenkins. Law gained Longstreet's ire after the battle of Wauhatchie for allegedly withdrawing too quickly. For Campbell's Station, thirty years later, Longstreet still blamed Law's "wrong movement" for costing him a victory. (aphcw)

be. Burnside handled his delaying actions well, and they proved critical before the Union troops finally headed for Knoxville on a long, arduous nighttime march.

If Longstreet's two division commanders were confused about the time of the attack, Longstreet must be held accountable. As a result of the infantry's confusion and Burnside's delaying action, the battle of Campbell's Station became chiefly an artillery duel between the two forces, as historian Earl Hess has noted. Even Longstreet's competent artillery commander, Porter Alexander, noted in his postwar works that "Had we had good maps of the country, we had it in our power to have cut off & capture a part of his troops, by pushing directly to Campbell's Station from our crossing; but, instead, we turned towards Lenoir. We arrived too late to attack & during the night the enemy retreated."

Jenkins placed the blame on "some mismanagement of General Law," which denied the Confederates a victory. Just as he had done after the battle of Wauhatchie, Longstreet once again backed Jenkins. Long after the sounds of battle fell silent, Longstreet still claimed that Law had "robbed him of a victory." However, even with much scrutiny surrounding the actions at Campbell's Station, the Confederate leadership initiated no inquiry or court-martial proceedings against Law, who refused responsibility for the loss at Campbell's Station. As one historian has put it: "Law's only defense against the rumor was his emphatic denial of the charge."

As Longstreet and Jenkins piled on the accusations against Law, Lafayette McLaws aimed verbal assaults against Longstreet. McLaws even wrote to Braxton Bragg that Longstreet failed to press Burnside with any vigor or sense of urgency. With Longstreet making, in McLaws's estimation, little to no effort to take either initiative or risk, "I therefore concluded and so did others, that [Longstreet] did not intend to make 'sudden blows' and his frequent unexplained delays, on the road up to this, had made it evident that 'rapid movements' were not in his program."

Casualties on both sides proved relatively light. Burnside suffered 318 casualties, 31 of them killed in action. On the Confederate side, McLaws never reported his casualty figures for the 16th; however, Jenkins noted his casualties amounted to 174 men. Local civilians in the area indicated 91 Confederates were killed and more than 300 wounded. Historian Earl Hess suggests "those numbers seem exaggerated."

At Campbell's Station

The Farragut Museum

FARRAGUT MUSEUM
ADMIRAL FARRAGUT COLLECTION

The Farragut Museum houses the Admiral David Glasgow Farragut collection. Admiral Farragut was born in this area in July 1801. In 2010, A Civil War Trails Historical Marker was placed in the Farragut Town Hall, commemorating the battle of Campbell's Station. (el)

9" DAHLGREN CANNON
FROM THE
USS HARTFORD

The USS *Hartford* served as Farragut's flagship during the August 1864 battle of Mobile Bay. This is one of the cannons from the *Hartford*. The U.S. government awarded twelve Medals of Honor to *Hartford* sailors for their actions during the battle. (el)

Since the battle of Chickamauga, Longstreet had been in near-constant disagreement with officers both subordinate and superior. The lack of success on the battlefield, the constant struggle for proper rations and clothing for his soldiers, and "blaming Law for the failure at Campbell's Station," said one pair of historians, "only demonstrated the depth of the crisis within Longstreet's command." The delays and lack of support from the Army of Tennessee before Longstreet's November departure from Chattanooga and continuing while enroute toward Knoxville "had sapped his initiative."

Burnside's performance at Campbell's Station demonstrated a clear understanding of his objective in

On the grounds of the Farragut Museum is a bronze statue of Admiral Farragut by sculptor Linda Rankin. Farragut was the first commissioned admiral of the United States Navy. He is best known for his statement—probably apocryphal—during the battle of Mobile Bay, "Damn the torpedoes, full speed ahead." (el)

drawing Longstreet further away from Chattanooga, not seeking a slugfest but enticing him along. Burnside ordered his men to break contact and seek out a second line about half a mile past the crossroads, "slowly withdrawing his troops, regiment by regiment, from the advanced position near the village." Brigadier General Edward Ferrero of the IX Corps's First Division described the delaying actions performed by Burnside's troops:

> *I have to state that never did troops maneuver so beautifully and with such precision as during the engagement; changing positions several times under a severe fire, it seemed more like a drill for field*

*movements than otherwise; brigades moving forward
to relieve each other, others retiring, having exhausted
their ammunition; changes of front, passing of defiles,
were executed by men and officers, so as to draw forth
exclamation of the highest praise by those who were so
fortunate as to behold their movements.*

It was for these reasons that Longstreet later complimented Burnside's performance in East Tennessee.

* * *

General Braxton Bragg assigned Maj. Gen. Joseph Wheeler (above) to Longstreet's command. While Wheeler was able to capture Maryville, Tennessee, he was unsuccessful in taking the heights south of Knoxville. (loc)

Amid operations leading up to Cambell's Station, Longstreet directed his cavalry element to move against the U.S. heights in Knoxville, south of the river. As directed by Longstreet on November 13, Maj. Gen. Wheeler took four brigades with a mission to capture the heights south of the river or to "threaten the enemy at Knoxville, so as to prevent his concentrating his forces against us before we reached Knoxville." If Wheeler could secure these heights, he could very well trigger the abandonment of the city and force Burnside into a precarious position between Longstreet and Confederate soldiers coming from the area of Virginia. If so, Longstreet might achieve his goal of facing Burnside in an open battle.

There, Wheeler ran into stiffer resistance from the inexperienced U.S. cavalrymen of the newly organized XXIII Corps manning Fort Dickerson. With the heights presenting too much of a challenge, Wheeler recognized any determined assault against the forts would prove suicidal.

Longstreet recalled Wheeler's cavalry and directed him to cooperate with his main force moving toward Knoxville. Wheeler rejoined Longstreet after the battle of Campbell's Station, on November 17.

In hindsight, Longstreet would have been better off if he had kept Wheeler with him throughout the Campbell's Station operation. Longstreet could have utilized Wheeler's cavalry to impede Burnside's movement toward Knoxville, disrupting his limited lines of communication back to Knoxville. While the mission he went on was potentially advantageous to Longstreet's overall strategy, Wheeler's efforts against the heights south of the city proved fruitless and, ultimately, meaningless. Burnside's engineers later established four earthworks critical to the overall defensive plan for the city. These forts were: Fort Higley, Fort Dickerson, Fort Stanley, and a smaller fort, Sevierville Hill (Fort Hill). Named after Capt. Jonathan C. Dickerson of the 112th Illinois Mounted Infantry, who died in action around Cleveland, Fort Dickerson proved the strongest of the four.

Increasingly cold, muddy, and weary, the soldiers of Burnside's command steadily withdrew from their positions along Campbell's Station once darkness settled. Burnside's destination was seventeen miles away: the expanding defensive network of Knoxville. Longstreet's men suffered from the same conditions, which also thwarted any attempt by the Confederates to close up and invite battle before Burnside reached Knoxville.

The lack of sleep over the preceding days had also taken its toll on both sides. Accounts exist of officers nodding off while in the saddle, and soldiers expressed with certainty that they slept while marching. Taking in little food, perhaps a piece of hardtack, one artillery officer allowed his men to take turns riding on the limbers, gaining what rest they could during the march. A Michigan soldier recalled it was "seventeen of the longest, weariest miles that it has ever been my misfortune to travel."

By November 17, most of Burnside's men staggered into Knoxville, wearied beyond words from the night's march. Though he was perhaps too exhausted to congratulate himself for his strategic retreat, Burnside's efforts drew praise from General Grant. "So far you are doing exactly what appears to me right," Grant wrote after the battle of Campbell's Station. "I want the enemy's progress retarded at every foot all it can be, only giving up each place when it becomes evident that it cannot be longer held without endangering your force to capture."

Burnside realized, however, he still needed a few days to complete the defenses in and around Knoxville. He had to delay the approaching Confederates for just a little longer. For this task, he turned to his competent and well-respected cavalry commander, Brig. Gen. William Sanders.

The battle of Knoxville was about to begin.

Fort Sanders

CHAPTER FIVE
NOVEMBER 17–NOVEMBER 23, 1863

A Kentuckian born in 1833, William Sanders moved to Natchez, Mississippi, when he was seven years old. His father's strong political connections as a lawyer helped Sanders secure a West Point appointment, where he graduated in 1856. When the war started, he saw service in Washington D.C., and by March 1863, he was colonel of the 5th Kentucky (Union) Cavalry. Burnside directed that Sanders conduct a raid into East Tennessee, working to disrupt Confederate communications and transportation assets. He also pursued John Hunt Morgan's raiders in July 1863. Sanders arrived back in Knoxville in early September, 1863.

Burnside came to respect and value Sanders's service. And as Burnside and his forces gathered inside Knoxville, Burnside called upon Sanders to stem the approach of the Confederates as he finalized the defenses inside the city.

Burnside tasked Sanders to hold back Longstreet's approaching columns. Sanders led his own 1,000-man brigade to the outskirts of Knoxville to meet

Known also as Confederate Memorial Hall, the Bleak House is owned and operated by the United Daughters of the Confederacy and was styled after a Tuscany villa. Robert Houston Armstrong built the house, naming it after an 1853 Charles Dickens novel. The house served as a headquarters for both Longstreet and McLaws. (el)

Most historians agree that one of the shots that killed Union General William P. Sanders came from this position at the Bleak House. The house and tower came under heavy Union fire. At least one of the Confederate soldiers died. An unknown soldier preserved the moment with a portrait. Bloodstains and bullet holes are still visible on the walls. (el)

the foe. Arrayed across the Kingston Road, Sanders positioned the 8th Michigan Cavalry on his left against the Holston River. The 112th Illinois Mounted Infantry held the center, and the 45th Ohio Mounted Infantry held the right flank. Two additional units, the 11th and 27th Kentucky Cavalry, provided coverage across the East Tennessee and Georgia Railroad to Sanders's right.

But even as Sanders's men deployed, Burnside called a conference at his headquarters, which Sanders attended. Also present at this late-night meeting on the 17th was Burnside's chief engineer and the officer strengthening Knoxville's defense, Capt. Orlando Poe. When pressed about how much time he needed to finish the defenses, Poe answered that he could complete the work by the next day, November 18. Burnside then turned to Sanders and asked if he could hold out that long. Burnside confidently ended the meeting when Sanders promised him he could.

Just one more day.

That day dawned with heavy fog, which restricted Confederate movements during the early morning hours. Longstreet intended to push the divisions of McLaws and Jenkins forward, forcing Sanders to give ground from his position.

By 10:00, Confederate sharpshooters in the Armstrong home opened fire. Just before noon, the Confederate infantry pressed forward, forcing back elements of the 45th Ohio Mounted Infantry. The U.S. forces, however, gathered their composure and steadied their lines. The Confederate skirmishers "resumed their work about 1 p.m. in preparation for a major push against Sanders." Porter Alexander soon complemented the infantry with four artillery pieces near the Armstrong home; Sanders, in contrast, was without any artillery support.

Porter Alexander later remarked that Sanders "held a line of rail breastworks on a hill near the Armstrong House, and interfered seriously with our freedom of motion."

Confederate artillery and infantry began to press, and the U.S. soldiers slowly began to give ground. Sanders, however, had made a promise to Burnside, and he intended to keep it. Captain Poe recalled that on November 18, Sanders mounted his white charger and rushed toward the rail piles to inspire his men. In the uncompleted defensive works behind them, seeing

William Sanders was born on August 12, 1833, in Frankfort, Kentucky. He graduated from West Point in 1856, finishing 41st in his class. Ironically, West Point superintendent Robert E. Lee almost dismissed Sanders from the academy, but he managed to remain at West Point with the assistance of the secretary of war, Jefferson Davis. (na)

This anchor and chain at the Bleak House were pulled out of the Tennessee River on December 18, 1962. Burnside's engineers placed this anchor and iron cable boom across the then-Holston River on November 23, 1863. (el)

Marker indicating the death of
Brig. Gen. William Sanders,
killed by Confederate
sharpshooters positioned in
the Bleak House not far from
this location. (el)

The final resting place for
Brig. Gen. William Sanders
at the Chattanooga National
Cemetery. (el)

their commander expose himself to the apparent dangers, the soldiers quelled their notions of retreat and stood fast. Sanders even directed the artillery to take out a contingent of Confederate sharpshooters that was playing havoc with his men. A well-aimed shot silenced the harassers, but not before one more U.S. soldier found himself on the receiving end of the Confederate snipers: William Sanders.

The doctors could do little to save the young officer. "Well, I am not afraid to die," Sanders replied when they informed him he was dying. "I have made up my mind upon that subject. I have done my duty and have served my country as well as I could."

Taken into the city for what care could be provided, Sanders died on November 19, about the same time President Lincoln was giving his famous Gettysburg Address.

Later that evening, officers gathered for a somber memorial service to remember the officer who had given them just enough time to complete their defenses. Many exhausted U.S. soldiers bitten by hard fighting recalled being awakened by subdued band music that drifted across the night air. Perhaps fittingly, one Confederate soldier remarked that as they approached the city, they could hear Federal bands striking up the

During the Civil War, this building was the Lamar House, and it was here that Brig. Gen. William Sanders died on November 19, 1863, after his wounding while delaying Confederate advances into Knoxville the day prior. Today, it is the Bijou Theater, located at 803 South Gay Street. (el)

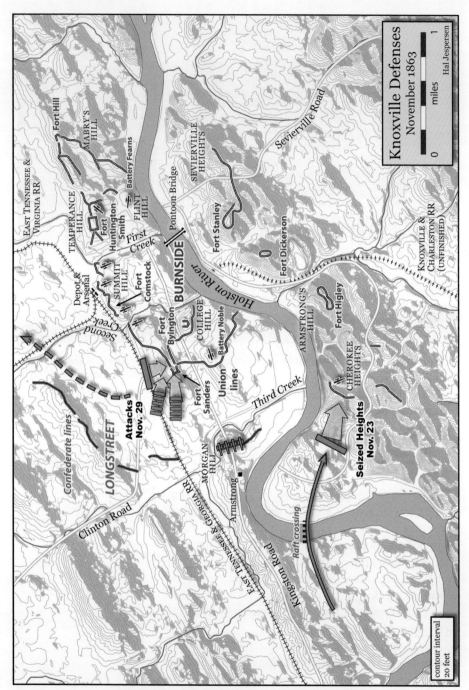

KNOXVILLE DEFENSES—Burnside and his engineers profited from the Confederate work accomplished under Simon Buckner prior to their occupation of the city in early September 1863. The Union forces completed their Knoxville defenses shortly after the battle of Campbell's Station on November 16, and Sanders's delaying action on November 18, 1863.

The city of Knoxville from across the Tennessee River. The future University of Tennessee is captured in this photograph, taken from the south bank of the Tennessee River. (loc)

notes of a tune often played by both sides, "When This Cruel War is Over." For William Sanders, the cruel war was over indeed.

*   *   *

According to census records, the population of Knoxville increased 155% from 1850 through 1860, reaching 5,600. The placement of the railroad through the city made it an inviting target for business expansion and growth. When war came, the railroad made it a strategic location for both the United States and the Confederacy.

Mabry Hill rose to the east, dominating two other hills in that part of the city, Flint and Temperance Hill. Rounding about to the north and continuing west, the University of East Tennessee sat on another plateau. "On the western approaches, Burnside enclosed his defensive line on the river and laid out a fortified line which ran north of the town until it almost reached the East Tennessee and Virginia Railroad," pointed out Morris Penny and J. Gary Laine, "where it then bent around the north of Knoxville."

IE   82

FORT DICKERSON

Linking with other hills south of the river, this Union position was a major factor in the defense of Knoxville. Occupied on Nov. 1, 1863, by the 2nd Brig. (Col. Daniel Cameron), 3rd Div. XXIII Corps, its gunfire broke up an attempt on Nov. 15-16 by Confederate cavalry which had come via Sweetwater and Maryville to seize these heights in Longstreet's bid to capture the city.

TENNESSEE   HISTORICAL   COMMISSION

Named after Capt. Jonathan C. Dickerson of the 112th Illinois Mounted Infantry, who was killed in action near Cleveland, Tennessee, Fort Dickerson was the first and most robust of the four forts built by U.S. engineers south of the river across from Knoxville. (el)

Strung out east to west, Knoxville rose 150 feet above the Holston River. High elevations both north and south of the river made prime targets for the Confederates.

If Longstreet occupied the heights south of the river, the Confederates could easily pummel the U.S. defenses across the river. Previously known as Fort Buckner, then Fort Loudon, and then taking on a name in honor of the recently-killed William Sanders, Fort Sanders took its sentinel position in the western part of Knoxville between the river and the railroad. As with the forts south of the river, should Longstreet take Fort Sanders, Burnside's position in Knoxville would become unsustainable.

Three creeks ran from the city down into the river, presenting slight obstacles to Longstreet's planning efforts. Occupying these grounds, Burnside could assemble around 12,000 men under arms in Knoxville, which included about 51 artillery pieces.

Longstreet headed north out of Chattanooga with very little intelligence on the topography of East Tennessee and, in particular, the area around Knoxville. Streams and rivers crisscrossed the region and could easily confuse a person unfamiliar with the surroundings. These peculiarities played a key role in Longstreet's struggle to suffocate Burnside in the besieged city. Longstreet met with several residents of Knoxville who were sympathetic to the Confederate cause to learn how he might starve Burnside into submission. Armed with a clear knowledge of the areas around Knoxville, the residents pointed out that the French Broad, a river flowing further east, was not patrolled by Confederate forces. Consequently, Burnside could float barges down the French Broad, where it linked up with the Holston River. The barges could then make the short ride into the city, under the cover of darkness.

Despite this intelligence, Longstreet trusted the maps in his possession, which insisted that the French Broad was several miles below Knoxville, near Lenoir's Station. One resident recalled that Longstreet "hooted at them and told them that they did not know what they were talking about or else were unfriendly to him and his cause." As a result, Burnside was able to bring some of the rich necessities from nearby counties into the city, undetected by Confederate patrols.

Burnside had also placed a 1,000-foot boom across the Holston River from which to fetch supplies provided by the loyal citizens of East Tennessee. The boom proved effective in catching rafts floating down the river. The assembled pontoon bridge served as a means to move food and provide communications to both sides of the river. As Grant pointed out in his memoirs, the Union loyalists "also drove cattle into Knoxville by the east side, which was not covered

Major General Simon Buckner was named Commander of the Department of East Tennessee and established his headquarters in Knoxville on April 27, 1863. He laid out some of the initial defensive works in Knoxville. (aphcw)

Instrumental in organizing and preparing the defenses in and around Knoxville, Orlando Poe graduated from West Point in 1856. After Knoxville, Sherman appointed Poe as his chief engineer. Poe oversaw much of the fall 1864 burning of Atlanta. After the war, Poe was responsible for many of the lighthouses constructed on the Great Lakes. (mhc)

by the enemy." Longstreet's ignorance of the terrain around Knoxville and his stubborn resistance to any contrary intelligence about the river networks allowed Burnside to receive much-needed sustenance.

With its supplies secure for now, the Union army set to finalize the city's defense, and the newly christened Fort Sanders became a prime object of their attention.

Confederate Brig. Gen. Danville Leadbetter, Bragg's chief engineer, had been the first to supervise the construction of the defensive works in the city. The Confederates had established the fort on the military crest of the western slope of the ridge, slightly below its topographical crest. This gave the defenders, now U.S. troops, several advantages, including direct observation and excellent fields of fire. There was also little dead space where an advancing enemy could take cover. And, critically, defenders would not be silhouetted against the sky. If the Confederates could take this most western of forts, Alexander and his guns would undoubtedly force Burnside's hand in either surrendering altogether or moving out of the city. Burnside and his engineers had worked hard to forestall this; when U.S. forces had first occupied the city in early September, Captain Poe and his team set to work to finalize the array of defenses in and around Knoxville.

Fort Sanders offered several distinct tactical advantages, improved by Poe's attention to detail. The U.S. constructed rifle pits to the front, ranging from 30 to 80 yards in advance of the Union positions. The soldiers also cleared the trees in front, leaving the landscape littered with tree stumps just over a foot high. To take further advantage of all of these stumps, the superintendent of the East Tennessee and Virginia Railroad offered several miles of rusted telegraph wire to Burnside and his men. With its rusty coloration, the wire was well camouflaged; Poe elected to wrap the wire around the dozens of stumps that surrounded Fort Sanders in the hopes of tripping up any advancing Confederate attack. Poe also took advantage of the creeks that flowed through the city, damming several, and creating ponds that prevented Longstreet from launching any attack on the north part of the city.

One Confederate offered the following description of Fort Sanders:

It was surrounded by a deep and wide moat, from the bottom of which to the top of the fort was from eighteen to twenty feet. In front of the moat for several hundred yards was felled timber, which formed an almost impassable abattis, while wire netting was stretched from stump to stump and around the fort. The creek that ran between our lines and the enemy's had been dammed in several places, forcing the water back to the depth of four to five feet. The fort was lined on three sides with the heaviest of field and siege pieces and crowded to its utmost capacity with infantry. This fort

The one-mile trail at High Ground Park takes one past rifle trenches and a cannon enclosure, part of the defensive network that was Fort Higley. (el)

Lieutenant Benjamin commanded the 2nd U.S. Artillery in Fort Sanders and was credited with firing the shot that took out Confederate snipers located at the Bleak House. (loc)

was on an acute angle of the line of entrenchments. From the right and left ran the outer or first line of breastworks, manned by infantry, and at every salient position cannons were mounted, completely encircling the entire city.

The builders of Fort Sanders "laid [it] out in strict accordance with the rules for constructing bastioned earthworks, but upon shorter exterior lines than were desirable," according to Poe. The northern and southern sides were 125 yards, the western side 95 yards, and the eastern side came in at 85 yards. The ditch was roughly twelve feet wide with a depth of six to eight feet, with a parapet rising another ten feet above the ditch. Poe estimated the U.S. had about 500 men inside Fort Sanders, supported by several cannons. These included four 20-pound Parrotts, six 12-pound Napoleons, and two 3-inch rifled guns, commanded by Lt. Samuel Benjamin.

It was no wonder the Confederates described Fort Sanders as a "formidable fortress."

Under the overall command of Brig. Gen. Edward Ferrero, soldiers of the 79th New York Infantry, 2nd Michigan Infantry, 29th Massachusetts Infantry, and the 20th Michigan manned the defenses of Fort Sanders. In his official report, Benjamin indicated he also drafted into service many African Americans to assist in building up the defenses. Their aid allowed the Federals to strengthen the fort's parapets, covering the cotton bales with rawhide to prevent musket fire from lighting them on fire. Since the Confederates had greater access to the woods around Knoxville, Poe's soldiers took the boards and shutters from the nearby college to build the revetments. The soldiers lined them with green bullock hides, to prevent splinters from flying around when struck.

Both the infantry and artillery officers realized they would have little time to react and get off good solid shots at the advancing Confederates before they were almost at the front steps of the fort. Lt. Benjamin understood that, under ideal conditions, cannoneers could get off perhaps two solid shots or three canister rounds every minute. Once they fired and then attempted to swab the guns with a wet sponge, his crews would be vulnerable to Confederate fire from

Brigadier General Edward Ferrero from New York commanded the First Division of the Ninth Corps under Ambrose Burnside during the East Tennessee Campaign. (loc)

close range. Benjamin would later manufacture grenades out of artillery shells, with three-second fuses to hurl at the Confederates as they advanced to the fort's perimeter. When the assault came, Benjamin laid out the grenades for easy access. Many of his soldiers appreciated the effect these weapons could have on the advancing enemy; however, some did wish "the damned things were somewhere else." The soldiers also had use of roman candles, to be fired into the air, allowing the visibility of the defenders to determine the direction of the Confederate attack.

For Longstreet a string of delays, some self-inflicted, some determined by weather, hindered his ability to strike a quick and decisive blow at Burnside. Growing threats in his rear from Grant in Chattanooga also served as a distraction to his planning. With December quickly approaching, Longstreet knew he must finish the job before both weather and events in Chattanooga overtook him.

"The Assault Must Be Tried"

CHAPTER SIX
NOVEMBER 24–NOVEMBER 27, 1863

"Our move was hurried," James Longstreet confessed in his memoirs. The limits on his transportation assets and pioneering tools stressed his corps' ability to meet even basic needs. To compensate, he sent a small contingent of cavalry south to Lenoir's Station to retrieve some of the tools they had confiscated there, which could be used to assist in making rifle pits for his sharpshooters.

Hurried as the move may have been, Porter Alexander recognized that every day that passed helped Burnside strengthen the Knoxville defenses. Even after a few days, Alexander noted, Burnside "had an interior line which might have successfully resisted, even had Fort Sanders been captured."

Historian Edward Hagerman, however, has concluded that Longstreet may not have been hurrying at all. While being pressed by Bragg, Longstreet

The Mabry-Hazen House is located at 1711 Dandridge Avenue in Knoxville. This home served as the headquarters for Confederate Brig. Gen. Felix Zollicoffer in the first year of the war. In the fall of 1863, the Mabry Home/Hill represented the eastern extension of Burnside's defenses in Knoxville. (el)

Soldiers from the 79th New York Highlander Regiment, 29th Massachusetts, and the 2nd and 20th Michigan Infantry supported the 2nd U.S. Regular Artillery, commanded by Lt. Samuel N. Benjamin. These soldiers manned the defenses at Fort Sanders. (loc)

was "less enthusiastic" to launch his own offensive, perceiving that he was being hurried into action. Lee's "Old Warhorse" never felt confident about rushing into an engagement and felt apparently even less so about this one.

Even those residents inside Knoxville sympathetic to the Confederate cause testified to their growing impatience for Longstreet to commence operations. "Longstreet advancing slowly—yet too slowly—upon the Federal army for he could save us now if he would press on them," observed Knoxville resident Elizabeth Baker Crozier in her diary. She wrote about "great excitement with the citizens during the siege which lasted about ten days during which time the authorities had every residence examined and the provisions taken into account, with the intention of confiscating them for the Yanks army, provided the siege continued. I have seen the soldiers beg for the scraps when the dishes were washed."

A 20th Georgia Infantry soldier, J. A. H. Granberry, echoed the young lady's sentiments. "If our army had followed the enemy right into the city without giving him time to fortify," the soldier wrote, "it was believed by many that the city, with the force that held it, would have been taken, but our gradual

A picture of Fort Sanders in 1864, facing west-northwest. The scene of Longstreet's assault on November 29, 1863. (loc)

approaches, occupying so many days, gave the enemy ample time to build new works and strengthen those already built." Frustration mounted, with both civilians and soldiers alike, waiting for the attack to commence.

On November 24, Longstreet ordered Law's Brigade to join Robertson's Texas Brigade south of the river. Longstreet wanted both brigades to make a demonstration "to ascertain the nature and location of its defenses as well as the force with which it was held." An aide to Longstreet, Maj. Osmun Latrobe, witnessed the demonstration and testified that a lack of support prevented success on this part of the battlefield. Subsequently, Longstreet ordered these commands to remain south of the river, awaiting further orders once the commander decided where to finally assault.

At Longstreet's urging, Bragg dispatched what historian Earl Hess called "surprisingly large reinforcements to Longstreet." The package included three infantry brigades and a battalion of artillery, all totaling nearly 4,000 men and twelve guns, under the command of Brig. Gen. Bushrod Johnson.

Bragg also committed to sending the aggressive Maj. Gen. Patrick Cleburne's division with Johnson, placing Cleburne in charge of all the reinforcements preparing to move to Longstreet. However, events then began to unfold in Chattanooga. Grant initiated his offensive against Bragg, capturing Orchard Knob on November 23, 1863. As a result, Bragg quickly recalled Cleburne and, in the end, only two brigades, around 2,600 soldiers, made their way to Longstreet.

*   *   *

Longstreet's artillery arm kept busy preparing for the assault, with Fort Sanders designated as their primary objective. Alexander had his thirty-four guns "posted in the most available positions to fire upon this fort and enfilade the adjacent lines." He positioned four howitzers—converted to mortars—to drop shells behind the U.S. lines. With Longstreet's approval, Alexander also ferried across rifled guns south of the river, positioned on a hill that offered a wide view of Burnside's position. However, even with their position looking down onto Fort Sanders, the guns were too far away to provide accurate and supporting fire. Repositioning a portion of Alexander's guns led to a delay in Longstreet's planned assault. Longstreet chose to wait for all forces to get positioned before initiating any offensive.

Longstreet delayed any offensive operation in Knoxville once he learned Bragg had dispatched forces from Chattanooga, including Ohio-born and 1840 West Point graduate Brig. Gen. Bushrod Johnson (above). (loc)

With a delay already caused by repositioning some of the artillery, Longstreet also paused until Johnson's force arrived from Chattanooga. It took Johnson four days to make the 115-mile journey. A slight bottleneck at the pontoon bridge in Loudon caused a day's delay, with supplies for the troops in Knoxville taking priority. Horses and all the empty wagons moved by road. The entire force did not report until just before the attack on Fort Sanders, which commenced on November 29.

Longstreet also withheld orders to advance when he received news of the arrival in Knoxville of Bragg's chief engineer, Brig. Gen. Danville Leadbetter. Leadbetter arrived shortly after dark on November 25. A native of Maine and an 1836 West Point graduate, Leadbetter brought with him a wealth of personal knowledge of the defenses in and around Knoxville. Leadbetter had supervised the original construction of the fort that became Fort Sanders when the Confederates held control of the

city. As historian Alexander Mendoza commented, Leadbetter's presence "seemed to calm [Longstreet]."

Leadbetter brought news to Longstreet that Bragg expected the commander to finish off Burnside quickly; events in Chattanooga were rapidly accelerating, with Grant's forces gaining strength with each passing day.

Riding with Longstreet on a reconnaissance, Leadbetter concluded that Fort Sanders presented such a formidable defense that it was not possible to attack it successfully, a view that caused additional delays for the assault. Further reconnaissance missions redirected the Confederate's gaze to Mabry Hill, a tall prominence on the opposite side of Fort Sanders to the east. With Mabry Hill established as the true target, a disheveled Porter Alexander spent an arduous period shifting his artillery to the new target.

And then the plan changed again. Another reconnaissance caused Leadbetter to shift his thinking again, back to Fort Sanders. While sensing a siege might be more successful, Longstreet recalled in his memoirs that Leadbetter informed him "the crisis was on, the time imperative and that the assault must be tried." An exhausted Alexander simply lamented, "General Leadbetter's advent cost us as three valuable days as the sun ever shone."

Further south, closer to Chattanooga, a cavalry action occasioned another pause in Longstreet's

Captain Orlando Poe and Col. Orville E. Babcock are here pictured at the defenses of Fort Sanders. Poe completed the defenses in and around Knoxville. Babcock later served on the staff of Lt. Gen. Ulysses S. Grant and delivered the terms of surrender to Gen. Robert E. Lee at the Appomattox courthouse in April 1865. (loc)

thinking. With ever-increasing lines of communication stretching from Knoxville to Chattanooga, Longstreet enjoyed little margin for error if he intended to dispose of Burnside and return swiftly back to Bragg. However, as military planners will always remind commanders in contingency forecasting, the enemy always has a vote.

For Longstreet, the unanticipated new factor turned out to be U.S. cavalry brigade commander Col. Eli Long. Long's brigade crossed the Tennessee River on November 24 and dashed toward Cleveland, Tennessee. "The telegraph was severed, and the railroad was destroyed in frequent places by burning and tearing up the track," Long wrote in his official report. Dividing his force to ensure that his men could do maximum damage to the infrastructure supporting the Confederates, Long then called off his raid on the 27th when pressed by Confederate cavalry. He returned to Chattanooga. While it may have been short in duration, historian David A. Powell commented that Long's raid "was largely responsible for preventing Longstreet from rejoining Bragg."

Further north, Longstreet finalized his assault plans on Fort Sanders. A final reconnaissance of Mabry Hill on November 27 seemed to convince him and Leadbetter that an assault on the position was impracticable. Upon their return back toward Fort Sanders, though, Longstreet noticed a soldier cross over the ditch in front of the fort. This observation convinced him that the ditch would not provide a formidable impediment to advancing troops after all. As Longstreet wrote after the campaign, "I was told by some officers that dogs were seen to pass over the same ditch. These circumstances led me to believe that the ditch on the west side was a slight obstacle." What Longstreet failed to consider, however, was that U.S. soldiers used planks when crossing the ditch. This oversight on Longstreet's part would have fatal consequences for his attack on Fort Sanders, which he scheduled for the afternoon of Saturday, November 28.

Alexander shuffled his artillery all around Knoxville as Longstreet and Leadbetter debated on the best location to assault. Once Longstreet decided on Fort Sanders, Alexander expressed supreme confidence. The initial plan was an assault "beginning

at sunrise," Alexander described, "and being preceded by a crushing fire of artillery concentrated on the fort and covered by an enveloping swarm of sharp-shooters." Given such a small target, there is little wonder Alexander expressed confidence that his artillery could have a decisive impact even before commanders issued orders for the infantry to advance.

However, Longstreet decided on a pre-dawn attack with minimal use of artillery; in essence, he decided that a surprise assault provided the best chance of success against Fort Sanders. The plan, as Longstreet explained in his official report, was as follows:

Three creeks ran through Knoxville down to the Holston River. U.S. forces dammed two of them, narrowing any avenues of approach for Longstreet should he attack. This view of the first dammed creek looks toward the west, with Knoxville over the hill. (mhc)

> *The attack upon the fort was ordered for the 28th, but in order to get our troops nearer the works the assault was postponed until the daylight of the 29th. The line of sharpshooters along our entire front was ordered to advance at dark to within good rifle range of the enemy's lines, and to sink rifle-pits during the night in its advanced position, so that the sharpshooters along our whole line might engage the enemy upon an equal footing, while our columns made the assault upon the fort.*

With Alexander's guns now playing a minimal role, Longstreet planned to have three brigades from McLaws's division lead the assault, with one in reserve.

Among the first joint meetings of the Civil War Union and Confederate veterans, the Reunion of the Blue and the Gray in Knoxville, Tennessee, was held October 8-9, 1890. This photograph was taken from the roof of the J. D. Cowan house near Cumberland Avenue, near the site of present-day Sophronia Strong Hall on the University of Tennessee campus. The tent seen at left was the "Monster Tent" that could seat 15,000. It was erected near the edge of the remains of Fort Sanders. (mhc)

Longstreet ordered Jenkins to have one brigade "pass the enemy's lines east of the fort, and to continue the attack along the enemy's rear and flank." The two brigades up from Chattanooga would move in the rear of McLaws's advancing troops, "thrown in as circumstances might require."

*   *   *

Just as Long's raid near Cleveland had disrupted Longstreet's ability to return to Chattanooga, Grant's movement on Orchard Knob in Chattanooga on November 23 (and Lookout Mountain the next day) proved a harbinger of ominous reports from Bragg. Longstreet got an initial warning of activity in Chattanooga on November 23, via telegraph. On November 26 and 27, Longstreet received "so many reports leading to the same conclusion that I determined that I must attack, and, if possible, get possession of Knoxville."

McLaws, planning the assault on Fort Sanders, pleaded with Longstreet to pause, he wrote, "until we hear the result of the battle of Chattanooga." McLaws even suggested that if Bragg had met defeat in Chattanooga, Longstreet should develop lines of communication with Virginia. However, Longstreet would hear nothing of it. Writing to McLaws on

November 28, Longstreet emphasized, "I am not at all confident that General Bragg has had a serious battle at Chattanooga. . . . This assault must be made at the time appointed and must be made with a determination which will insure success. . . . It is a great mistake to suppose that there is any safety for us in going to Virginia if General Bragg has been defeated."

If the situation in Chattanooga was growing increasingly dark for Bragg, Burnside was relaying to Grant that his situation was becoming equally dire. Writing to Grant on November 23, Burnside shared, "Our defenses are comparatively strong, the men in good spirits; we have provisions for, say, ten or twelve days longer, and will hold out as long as we can." Burnside had cut in half rations of bread and meat to his men. And it was not long afterward that he had to withhold coffee and sugar completely, even with the provisions that the loyal citizens around Knoxville had provided to them via the French Broad River.

And what supplies Burnside could collect outside those cast down the river were from wagon trains, a supply hub located 160 miles away at Camp Nelson in Kentucky. With high mountain ranges to cross and an arduous journey for both soldiers and animals, "[o]ne man counted 114 dead mules during one day travel along the route in November 1863," noted historian Earl Hess. One soldier from Indiana concluded, "Any thinking man could have seen that it was absolutely impossible to supply an army in East Tennessee by wagons over the mountains."

With the situation getting tense in Chattanooga, Bragg directed Longstreet to return Maj. Gen. Wheeler back to Chattanooga on November 23. As Wheeler stated in his official report, "I turned the command over to General Martin, and started in compliance with said order."

Wheeler's departure, the growing rumors emanating from Chattanooga, the dwindling supply issue, and the pressure mountinig to return to Bragg only heightened Longstreet's awareness that he needed to act quickly against Burnside. Longstreet settled on Sunday, November 29 for the pre-dawn assault on Fort Sanders.

IE   69
FORT SANDERS

Fort Sanders, a bastioned earthwork on the ridge two blocks north of here, was the scene of Gen. James Longstreet's unsuccessful assault upon the Federal defenses of Knoxville at dawn, Nov. 29, 1863.

TENNESSEE HISTORICAL COMMISSION

"A Dismal Failure"

The Assault on Fort Sanders

CHAPTER SEVEN

NOVEMBER 28–DECEMBER 5, 1863

For Longstreet's commanders charged with the assault on Fort Sanders, they would have to rely on sheer courage and determination. There was hope for success, and that is what they counted on going forward.

However, Brig. Gen. Micah Jenkins grew increasingly anxious about the assault, especially after his conversation with the newly arrived Brig. Gen. Archibald Gracie. Gracie had first-hand knowledge of the fort's layout, including the depth of the ditch and the heights of the parapet. And everyone knew Burnside had been feverishly adding to the defensive network since his occupation of Knoxville in early September.

So disturbed was Jenkins at what Gracie relayed to him that Jenkins traveled to Longstreet's headquarters on November 28 to express his concerns. With Longstreet unavailable, Jenkins met with McLaws. Emphasizing the need for ladders or fascines to carry the heights, McLaws indicated he knew nothing of such matters and that "they would trust to luck in getting around or over."

Little evidence of Fort Sanders exists today, covered up by commercial development and the University of Tennessee. The Fort Sanders historical marker is located in proximity to where the fort once stood. (el)

After nightfall and still harboring deep anxieties, Jenkins met and discussed the situation with the weary Porter Alexander. Jenkins hoped that Alexander would ride with him to Longstreet's headquarters to convince the commanding general to provide ladders to the men, but Alexander demurred. Indicating weariness from the labor conducted in preparation for the attack, Alexander simply nodded concurrence with Jenkins's concerns and headed for his camp to rest.

Jenkins elected to write Longstreet, indicating what both McLaws and Gracie had relayed to him. But Longstreet still exuded confidence that the ditch and parapets would prove no formidable obstacle to his veterans. Longstreet wrote back to Jenkins and concluded with a hopeful statement: "If we go in with the idea that we shall fail, we will be sure to do so. But no men who are determined to succeed can fail." Longstreet was resting almost everything on hope.

Longstreet believed that securing the rifle pits in front of the fort and then launching a pre-dawn assault would surprise the Federal defenders. However, preparation for such an assault was bound to attract attention. A U.S. soldier from the 79th New York Highlanders took notice of such preparation. "During the afternoon," the soldier wrote, "the enemy was observed moving large bodies of troops toward our right. Their lines had approached closer in that direction on the west front of the fort, and we looked for an assault in that direction. Night closed in without any demonstration, but no one was allowed to sleep." Longstreet's preparatory movements had lost any chance of surprise; Burnside's men were ready.

Civil War veteran and historian of Kershaw's Brigade, Augustus Dickert, called it "the forlorn hope." The brigades of Bryan and Wofford's Georgians and the Mississippians of Humphreys would lead the way. Longstreet positioned the brigades of Kershaw and Anderson within easy supporting distance should the need arise. Porter Alexander explained that "a rapid fire by both guns and mortars, thirty-four in all, would begin, concentrated upon the fort as long as seemed necessary." The cessation of firing would be the signal for the infantry to assault in columns of regiments.

Private James Barrow of Cobb's Legion Infantry made an astute observation, belying his tender nineteen years, concerning the assault on Fort Sanders and Longstreet's insistence it must not fail:

> *McLaws was the Longstreet and Longstreet was the Lee of Gettysburg. Longstreet now was as determined as Lee had been at Gettysburg to attack. Whether this was because his subordinate dared question his strategy we do not know. He put McLaws in exactly the same position as Lee had placed him. Longstreet developed the strategy and told McLaws to develop and execute the tactics.*

Upon his arrival from Chattanooga, Archibald Gracie provided information on the Fort Sanders defenses to Longstreet's command. The information, however, went unheeded by the chain of command, including the ditch's specifications that surrounded the fort. (loc)

Longstreet's attack amounted to just over 6,000 soldiers, almost 41 percent of his infantry positioned around Knoxville. Lafayette McLaws led Longstreet's main effort with two columns: one led by Col. Solon Ruff commanding Wofford's brigade and another consisting of Brig. Gens. Benjamin Humphreys's and Goode Bryan's men. George T. Anderson's brigade positioned itself just to the north of the fort. The two brigades under Brig. Gen. Bushrod Johnson, led by Brig. Gen. Archibald Gracie and Col. John Fulton, were to the rear, ready to drive in with support as needed. Brig. Gen. Joseph Kershaw's brigade would advance on the right and take the trenches to its front once the Confederates took the fort. As historian Earl Hess noted, "Now that [Longstreet] had committed himself to an assault, [he] did not spare troops to do it."

Preliminary efforts by Longstreet's men included capturing Federal pickets and rifle pits outside the fort. This occurred in the early morning hours of November 29. It also confirmed to the forces in and around Fort Sanders that something was afoot. Writing on Burnside's East Tennessee Campaign, Henry Burrage, a member of the 36th Massachusetts, wrote:

> *It was now evident that Longstreet intended to make an attack at some point in our entrenched position. But where? All the remainder of that long, cold night— our men were without overcoats largely—we stood in the trenches pondering that question. Might not this demonstration in front of Fort Sanders be only a feint designed to draw our attention from other parts of the line where the principal blow was to be struck? So some thought. Gradually the night wore away.*

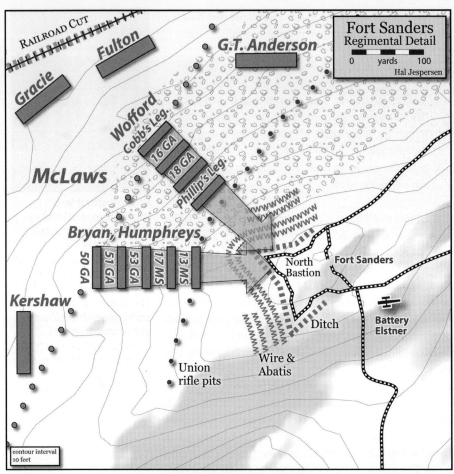

FORT SANDERS—The direction of attack showing the assault on Fort Sanders, November 29, 1863. The Confederates failed to breach the salient, finding themselves trapped in a ditch that surrounded the bastion.

With initial moves made and Alexander's guns, as he put it, firing merely "to encourage the storming columns, and . . . discontinued in a few minutes," Longstreet's men prepared to move out.

A young soldier from the 21st Mississippi Infantry described the scene just before moving toward Fort Sanders. "My eyes were watery from cold," Edward Burruss noted, "but this became more so from deeper cause as I looked down the line of half-clothed, less than half-shod heroes & saw their knees actually smiting together & their teeth rustling like dry bones." J. B. Polley of Hood's Texas brigade remembered that "It was so cold that even after running up the hill half a mile the men had to warm their fingers at the fires left

The fighting at Fort Sanders on November 29, 1863 was close-quarters combat during Longstreet's siege of Knoxville. Soldiers often used their rifles as clubs, even using axes to attack their foe. (mhc)

by the Yankees before they could reload their guns." Another soldier from the 21st Mississippi, J. B. Boothe, recalled the lines formed in preparation "almost as silent as a funeral procession." Called to attention, the soldiers fixed bayonets and moved forward. Yet, Longstreet directed the men to move forward without firing a shot; speed was of the essence, and Longstreet still hoped to spring a surprise

Neither a rebel yell nor a bullet pierced the air as the men moved forward to the fort, save for the shots from Confederate sharpshooters toward any U.S. soldier who poked his head up over the defenses. As Augustus Dickert described, Fort Sanders "was to be taken by cold steel alone." Longstreet and the senior commanders did not want any soldiers to pause and reload while moving across the open fields. It took a soldier eleven steps to reload, aim, and discharge their weapon, which would expend valuable time. Instead, commanders wanted their soldiers fully loaded and prepared to fire once they breached the initial defense and found themselves inside the fort.

The men in Fort Sanders were well prepared to receive the assault. The soldiers rotated shifts to maintain watch, sleeping at their positions along the defenses. Once the alarm sounded, "[t]he garrison was at once ready for an attack," Federal artillerist Lt. Samuel Benjamin emphasized in his official report. Peering into the darkness and huddled against the

dropping temperatures, the U.S. soldiers waited as the Confederates moved from their positions and drew closer.

Byron Cutheon of the 20th Michigan described the minutes spent anticipating the attack as Longstreet's veterans moved forward. "Never was an assault more gallantly or persistently delivered," Cutheon wrote, "and never one more completely and decisively repulsed."

The days of preparation leading up to the assault vanished almost immediately once the assault commenced. In near disgust, artillerist Porter Alexander lamented "[t]he advantages sacrificed for the illusive merits of a night attack." Moving in columns of regiments, grappling with the darkness, the columns invariably converged, the nature and lay of the land playing a role as the commands intermingled. Alexander explained that "officers could no longer separate or distinguish their own men."

Many Confederate and U.S. officers, Longstreet included, had received their formal military education at the United States Military Academy at West Point on the banks of the Hudson River. Dennis Hart Mahan, a long-standing prewar instructor on military tactics and operations, had always emphasized the importance of proper planning when attacking a structure such as the one Longstreet faced at Fort Sanders. Several demonstrations should be made at various points "to divert the attention of the assailed from the true point of the attack, and prevent him from concentrating his strength at that point." Mahan also indicated having "light scaling ladders, planks, fascines, strong hurdles, etc., for the purpose of descending into the ditch; to mount the scarp." Unfortunately, Mahan's lessons were largely forgotten during the attack on Fort Sanders.

The wire entanglements wrapped around the tree stumps proved to have little effect on the advancing Confederates. It failed to slow up Longstreet's men, described by historian Earl Hess as a "momentary delay." While perhaps befuddling the men in the front ranks, the mass of men simply crushed the wire to the ground, whereas the men in the middle and rear ranks took little notice of it. The ditch, wrapped around the northwest bastion, was a completely different story.

Confederate commander Brig. Gen. Benjamin Humphreys stated he and others believed the ditch would prove little hindrance to the men as they approached the fort. "The existence of the ditch was gravely doubted by many that professed to reconnoiter the works," Humphreys recalled, "and it was positively asserted that if the ditch existed at all, it was too slight to offer any impediment to any assaulting party." This was the prevailing opinion amongst the officers and men carrying out the assault. The result, reported one war correspondent, was a "scene of confusion" and a "discordance of pandemonium."

A January 1864 *Harper's Weekly* showing the assault on Fort Sanders with vicious hand-to-hand fighting taking place. (ga)

Once down in the ditch, the soldiers had few resources to scale the heights. The U.S. soldiers had saturated the walls with water, causing them to freeze, making it only harder for Confederates to gain the heights. One officer from the 13th Mississippi Infantry used his sword to carve notches in the wall, helping soldiers gain footholds to pull themselves up. In other places, soldiers were simply unable to climb, instead sliding back down into the growing puddles of blood accumulating at the bottom of the ditch. In some places, the blood was shoe-top deep. "The deep moat is finally almost literally bridged with human bodies," recalled one Southerner.

As Confederates piled up in the ditch, the Federals firing from above had no difficulty locating targets. One soldier of the 79th New York Infantry remembered, "There was no need to take careful aim; the brave rebels crowded up to the ditch, as the first line had done, and almost every bullet fired by us found a death mark. Shells were bursting in the ditch, literally tearing the poor fellows limb from limb and scattering the fragments far and near."

Pre-made hand grenades tossed over the walls created more chaos for the Confederates. Sergeant Major Granberry of the 20th Georgia Infantry admitted hand grenades, coupled with the lack of provisions to scale the walls, caused "panic and a retreat" in the Confederate soldiers.

In less than half an hour, the assault was over. Very few of Longstreet's veterans made it up and across the walls. U.S. soldiers captured at least three regimental flags: the 16th Georgia and two regimental flags from Mississippi, the 13th and 17th Infantry. The officer carrying the 16th Georgia flag found himself on top of the parapets, resting his hand on the muzzle of the cannon and demanding the U.S. soldiers surrender. The gunners quickly answered and blew the officer to pieces, the flag falling gently down into the fort.

The question now facing Longstreet was whether he should send in reinforcements, with the hope that additional troops might carry the fort. Some of his commanders pleaded for such support.

Mississippi soldiers carried this flag, the 17th Mississippi Regimental flag, during their assault on Fort Sanders. (mdah)

Longstreet had accompanied the brigades of Brig. Gen. Bushrod Johnson during the assault. Johnson patiently waited for Longstreet's signal to move forward and support the main body of troops assaulting the bastion. However, Longstreet received a report from one of McLaws's staff officers, Maj. James Goggin. Longstreet knew Goggin from their days together at West Point and had a healthy respect for his perspective. Goggin submitted that any further assaults on the fort were futile. As Longstreet put it in his memoirs, "[W]ithout a second thought I ordered the recall, and ordered General Johnson to march his brigades back to their camps." Longstreet also quickly called off the movement of Brig. Gen. Micah Jenkins.

Though Longstreet would later indicate a regret in issuing the recall notice, the assault on Fort Sanders was effectively over. Longstreet lamented after the war, "[C]onfidence in the conduct of the war was broken." Left behind were scores of Confederate dead and wounded.

*   *   *

As part of the operations on November 29, Longstreet intended for the brigades of Evander Law and Jerome Robertson to make efforts against U.S. fortifications south of the river. As happened in the main effort at Fort Sanders, the U.S. forces matched against these Confederate brigades enjoyed advantages of terrain and firepower. Consequently, this action also failed to achieve any success.

When Law pressed Longstreet as to whether he should continue after the Fort Sanders repulse, Longstreet simply directed a retirement to their original positions. Lee's "Old Warhorse," however, did give the Texas and Alabama brigades "credit for holding Federal troops south of the river who were designated as reserves for the garrison in Fort Sanders." Yet, an appendum to Longstreet's official report complimented neither Law nor Robertson in order to "further the case Longstreet was building against McLaws." Confederate casualties south of the river on November 29 were minuscule, quite the opposite of where Longstreet's main effort took place.

Porter Alexander put the Confederate casualties at just over 800 in the action at Fort Sanders, with 129 killed, 458 wounded, and 226 captured. Remarkably, the U.S. only sustained around twenty casualties.

At about noon on the 29th, Burnside granted a truce so that the dead and wounded soldiers could be collected. Just hours before, U.S. and Confederate soldiers had been in a desperate and vicious battle. Now, those same soldiers assisted each other in caring for the wounded. One U.S. soldier described taking Confederate bodies, stiffened by rigor mortis and the cold, and standing them up against the blood-stained walls of the ditch.

Burnside had turned away some of the best soldiers the Confederacy could assemble. Among their numbers were veterans of many battlefields who had often marched away in victory. Longstreet's veterans now had to withdraw to an uncertain future for his command.

For Lafayette McLaws, the reasons for the failure were clear. He identified the "slipperiness of the parapet, upon which it was impossible for any large body of men to gain a foothold and the severe fire from the north side of the fort, which drove the men from the most accessible point of ascent." "I do not think that ladders would have been of material assistance," McLaws added, "unless they had been furnished in great numbers and had been 20 feet long. The reconnaissance was also defective, giving false notions of the character of the work and of the ditch."

A half-hour after the repulse, Longstreet got disheartening news about Bragg. A telegram from President Davis indicated that Grant had defeated Bragg in Chattanooga, pushing the Army of Tennessee south toward Georgia. Longstreet received additional guidance to join Bragg's army in Dalton, Georgia. If that proved impractical, Longstreet should make his way back to Virginia. The decision was his to make. With a destination of Dalton, Georgia, in mind, Longstreet made initial preparations to move out, getting the soldiers ready to depart after nightfall. However, as Longstreet soon realized, the laborious mountainous route, disruption of rail services, and the long movement made departing Knoxville impossible. For the time being, Longstreet's First Corps would remain in East Tennessee.

Like spectres, Confederates advanced against Fort Sanders through a field of stumps with telegraph wire strung between them, as depicted in a painting on display in the University of Tennessee's McClung Museum of Natural History and Culture. (mhc)

However, with Bragg retreating into Georgia, Grant in Chattanooga wanted Burnside—and Longstreet—to know that help was on the way to Knoxville. Grant dispatched two riders carrying orders that support for Burnside—both infantry and cavalry—was coming from various directions. Grant intentionally sent one of the riders into Confederate hands to be sure Longstreet knew of the Federal commander's plans.

Longstreet spent the first days of December holding councils with his commanders. All concurred that a movement toward Bristol, Virginia, was the best course of action, going into winter quarters somewhere northeast of Knoxville. On December 2, the Confederates captured Grant's dispatch rider (as intended). This persuaded Longstreet that he now had no choice about moving out of Knoxville.

*   *   *

On December 2, Longstreet informed Bragg of the repulse at Fort Sanders, further letting the commander know that he was changing his supply depot "from Loudon to some point in the direction of Virginia." And in response to news that U.S. forces were converging on Knoxville, Longstreet prepared to withdraw closer to the Old Dominion. In First Corps General Order

Located on 17th Street, the United Daughters of the Confederacy (UDC) dedicated this monument in 1914 to soldiers who took part in the assault on Fort Sanders. (el)

No. 9, written on December 4, Longstreet directed that "The movement must be conducted with the utmost care and quietude. Officers will be particularly careful to have the usual camp fires built before night, but no more."

Following Longstreet's directive, the soldiers collected as much wood as they could to build glowing campfires. The night of December 4 proved clear and cold when Longstreet's soldiers quietly stepped out from their positions and headed away from Knoxville. Another fine opportunity had been lost. Historian James Coker referred to the campaign in Knoxville as "a series of good plans spoiled by unavoidable mishaps." Perhaps. Yet, Longstreet and his commanders had it in their grasp to quickly assault the defenses around Knoxville shortly after the battle of Campbell's Station, when U.S. forces were still catching their breath after that long march into the city.

Longstreet confided to President Davis on December 6 that his ammunition was getting low and his "force too weak to venture to hold against the enemy's forces approaching at various directions. . . . My transportation and supplies are not in condition to warrant any such hope now."

From the U.S. perspective, Orlando Poe best summarized the operations around Knoxville:

> *The siege of Knoxville passed into history. If mistakes were made in the defense, they were covered by the cloak of success. . . . The results of the successful defense are: The defeat of Bragg's army and consequent permanent establishment of our forces in Chattanooga, with tolerably secure lines of communication; the confirmation of our hold upon East Tennessee; the discomfiture of and loss of prestige by the choicest troops of the enemy's service.*

Both Burnside and Longstreet prepared for the next phase of operations.

Drive Longstreet as Far as You Can

CHAPTER EIGHT
DECEMBER 6–DECEMBER 14, 1863

Writing to Grant on December 6, Burnside confided that both the infantry and artillery were in no condition to follow the withdrawing Confederate forces. The operations in Knoxville over the past two weeks had greatly fatigued the army "by constant work in the trenches." Only his cavalry, Burnside concluded, might be fit to pursue Longstreet, and he dispatched Brig. Gen James Shackelford's horsemen to the chase. He then placed Maj. Gen. John Parke in command of the infantry to follow Shackelford. Burnside himself stayed in Knoxville, feeling the effects of ill health.

If Federal troops felt as prostrate as their commander, the retreating Confederates were faring worse. Historian William Marvel stated both armies "crawled like two great delegations of peasants, on their way to petition opposing emperors." Both forces struggled with the basic necessities of supplies and food, for men and horses.

Grant, however, remained hopeful that soon-to-arrive-reinforcements could be used to "crush Longstreet's forces or drive them from the valley," as

A monument to U.S. soldiers, unveiled in 1901 at the Knoxville National Cemetery. An eight-foot marble U.S. Soldier adorns the top of the monument. (el)

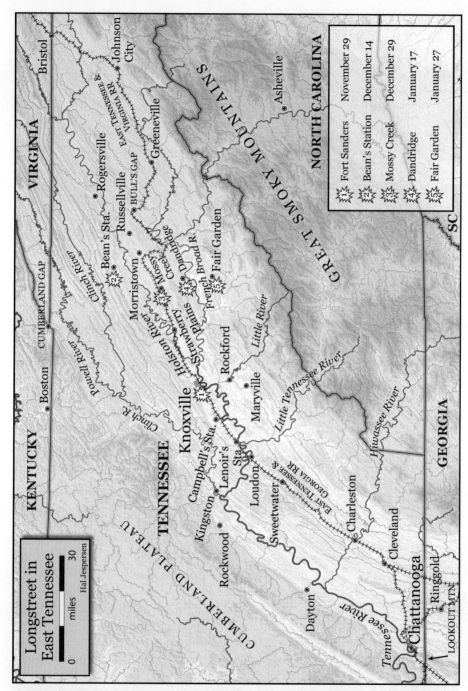

LONGSTREET IN EAST TENNESSEE—A series of engagements cultivated the East Tennessee landscape in the winter of 1863-1864. Cold weather, approaching Union reinforcements to Knoxville, and depletion of cavalry assets from his command pushed Longstreet further into East Tennessee.

he had written to Burnside at the end of November. Those reinforcements were led by Grant's dependable subordinate from previous campaigns, Maj. Gen. William T. Sherman. While Sherman and Grant's relationship went back to many joint adventures, Sherman was not exactly pleased to find himself venturing into East Tennessee.

With Burnside sending dispatches to Grant that supplies were running low during the siege, Grant took notice. "I immediately turned my attention to relieving Knoxville," Grant later wrote, "about the situation of which the President, in particular, was very anxious." Sherman's men, not far removed from a long trip to Chattanooga from Mississippi, were swiftly redirected to a 115-mile journey to Knoxville. With only a few days' rations, almost no change of clothes and, if lucky, a coat or blanket per man, Sherman's men headed out. "Recollect that East Tennessee is my horror," a displeased Sherman stressed to Grant on December 1. "That any military man should send a force into East Tennessee puzzles me. Burnside is there and must be relieved, but when relieved I want to get out, and he should come out too." Regardless, Grant well knew the importance of East Tennessee to President Lincoln. Sending Sherman off to Knoxville reflected that awareness.

Newspaper publisher and influential East Tennessee Unionist William Brownlow urged Lincoln in a November 30 letter to consolidate the gains recently made in East Tennessee. Brownlow also praised the efforts of Burnside. He called Burnside a "military hero, and deserved everlasting honors." Brownlow's biographer, E. M. Coulter, pointed out that the interest of East Tennessee "had been a question of sentiment, politics, and military strategy inexplicably bound up." It was for these reasons that Lincoln consistently reminded Grant to always remember Burnside— proxy for East Tennessee's loyalists—when developing his strategy for the region. Grant's move to send Sherman northward to support Burnside certainly met with Lincoln's approval.

One Confederate soldier recalled William "Parson" Brownlow "explicitly showed them the follies of Secession that the Devil was the first secessionist and that the spirit was as wicked as it was unjust." Brownlow became Tennessee's governor just before the war ended. He died on April 29, 1877 and is buried in Knoxville's Old Gray Cemetery. (el)

"I sent word to General Sherman of the situation," Grant wrote in his memoirs, "and directed him to march to the relief of Knoxville. I also gave him the problem that we had to solve—that Burnside had now but four or five days supplies left, and that he must be relieved within that time." Grant confided to General in Chief Henry Halleck that he trusted "Sherman's promptness and ability."

Sherman's robust relief force from Chattanooga included the IV Corps with Maj. Gen. Gordon Granger and Maj. Gen. Phil Sheridan. Sherman also brought up the XI and XV Corps. Recognizing that their "fellow soldiers were beleaguered in the mountain town of Knoxville," Sherman urged the relief force onward, gathering whatever food they could on the side of the road. The soldiers, Sherman concluded, "were ill-supplied for such a march." However, on December 6, Sherman arrived in Knoxville, with Granger arriving later in the day.

Sherman was impressed by what he saw when he examined Knoxville's fortifications. He called it, "a wonderful production for the short time allowed in their selection of ground and construction of work."

Upon returning from his tour of the defenses, Sherman and his officers sat down for a dinner, compliments of Ambrose Burnside. "There was a regular dining-table, with clean table-cloth, dishes, knives, forks, spoons, etc.," Sherman recalled in his memoirs. It was an extravagant display, and Sherman took some offense. Burnside had previously stated his army was short of food and supplies. Shown such luxuries, Sherman observed, "Had I known this, I should not have hurried my men so fast; but until I reached Knoxville, I thought his troops there were actually in danger of starvation."

Confronted by Sherman over the dinner display, "Burnside sheepishly admitted that his situation had never been as bad as it had seemed," according to Sherman biographer John Marszalek. Taking an opposing view, Burnside biographer William Marvel stated the Army of the Ohio commander simply neglected to inform Sherman of the effort it took to provide a satisfactory dinner evening for his guests.

As Sherman and Burnside conversed, Burnside expressed appreciation for Sherman's promptness but

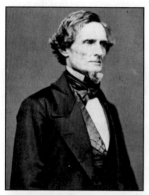

The president of the Confederacy, Jefferson Davis, should have been the ideal commander-in-chief, as he was a West Point graduate and served as secretary of war in the Franklin Pierce administration. However, he proved to be less effective than Abraham Lincoln in this role. (loc)

intimated that he did not require such a large force in Knoxville. He also expressed concern that Bragg might resume the offensive. If Sherman needed to, Burnside said, he was welcome to about-face and head back to Chattanooga.

Sherman was more than happy to take Burnside up on his offer, and he took the occasion to solve another nagging problem: Sherman left the lackadaisical Granger and his two IV Corps divisions in support of Burnside, much to Granger's disgust. As historian David A. Powell pointed out, Granger's men were so short of supplies that Burnside left them in Knoxville while he prepared to pursue Longstreet. Granger and "his men were now marooned in East Tennessee and destined for yet more living on short rations."

Bean's Station was founded in the late 18th Century. Union soldiers of the 27th Kentucky Mounted Infantry took up defensive positions at the Bean's Station hotel during the battle on December 14, 1863. (tslc)

* * *

Difficulties followed Longstreet's men as they moved away from Knoxville. Writing to President Davis on December 6, Longstreet stated he planned to position his command somewhere around Bean's Station "with the hope of getting an opportunity to strike the enemy's column that might attempt to

Major General Burnside retained Gordon Granger while the rest of Sherman's troops departed Knoxville for Chattanooga. Granger is probably best remembered for issuing General Order No. 3 on June 19, 1865 in Galveston, Texas. The order informed the residents of President Lincoln's Emancipation Proclamation issued two years earlier. June 19 is now commemorated as a federal holiday known as Juneteenth. (loc)

approach the Cumberland Gap, and if he should pursue me from Knoxville, to destroy my force."

However, Longstreet also offered a bleak operational assessment to the president:

> *My transportation and supplies are not in condition to warrant any such blow. The roads are getting to be almost impassable, and, to increase our difficulties, many of our men are without shoes. If I should have an opportunity, I shall not fail to improve it. I presume that I shall be obliged to make my way slowly back to Virginia.*

Both officers and men did what they could to sustain themselves. Fences and barns stood little chance with soldiers looking for warmth and shelter in the neighborhood. Many East Tennesseans fled the area as soldiers confiscated whatever livestock they came across. Reflecting sheer desperation, soldiers stripped the window sashes and sewer piping of lead. Even moonshiners were not left out, soldiers taking the copper tubing used to produce their spirits. The soldiers took it all for the good of the war effort.

As Confederates scoured the countryside for food and supplies, U.S. forces organized themselves for the next operational phase. Even as they did so, Lincoln finally approved the leave Burnside had applied for at the end of October. Burnside had cited lingering health concerns, but Lincoln had declined the request because of the uncertain situation in East Tennessee. Now, as Longstreet limped out of Knoxville and with the city secure and U.S. forces growing in strength, Lincoln finally honored Burnside's request.

In fact, Lincoln was so pleased with how events had turned out that, on December 7, he urged the people of the north to "assemble at their places of worship and render special homage to Almighty God for this great advancement of the national cause." Both houses of Congress passed a resolution giving thanks to Ambrose Burnside and the men under his command while in East Tennessee—an event that occurred only a handful of times during the war.

Burnside's performance in command of the army in East Tennessee revived his tarnished military reputation, which had taken a significant hit after his brief tenure in command of the Army of the Potomac. "[Burnside's] subsequent conduct during the siege of Knoxville restored him to the full confidence of the administration," concluded historian Oliver Temple.

Taking Burnside's place in command in Knoxville was an old friend from Burnside's days during the North Carolina campaign, Maj. Gen John Foster, who arrived on December 11. Burnside departed the next day.

Grant's directives to Foster were simple: "Drive Longstreet to the farthest point east you can. Retain Granger as long as may be necessary." Foster responded by enumerating the obstacles he faced, from harsh weather conditions, scarcity of supplies, and the infantry in poor condition, to difficult terrain. "These obstacles," he wrote to General Halleck and Grant on December 12, "interfere very much with my desire to move up in force and engage Longstreet, where he may halt, and may render it impossible in a short time." Foster protested again the following day to Halleck and Grant, preferring "to wait a while before advancing in force."

Major General John G. Foster took over from Ambrose Burnside in mid-December 1863. Foster was a major assigned under Maj. Robert Anderson at Fort Sumter in Charleston, South Carolina, when the fort fell in April 1861. Three years later, Foster returned to regain Fort Sumter and Charleston. (loc)

Meanwhile, Confederate President Jefferson Davis was making command changes of his own. After the retreat from Chattanooga to Dalton, Georgia, Braxton Bragg submitted his resignation to Davis. Perhaps to Bragg's surprise, Davis accepted, and Bragg turned over temporary command of the army to William Hardee on December 2. Joseph Johnston would eventually command the army, leading it through most of the Atlanta Campaign. Two months later, Bragg reported to Richmond and would serve as Davis's military advisor.

On December 10, Davis named Longstreet a department commander, taking command of all troops in East Tennessee. This new authority seemed to embolden Longstreet, who readied himself "to turn and strike his enemy," according to historian Earl Hess. As long as Longstreet remained in the area, the threat he represented to East Tennessee posed a problem for the Union. From a military point of view, Longstreet threatened Grant's flank and rear at Chattanooga. He also endangered the peace and safety of the loyal citizens of East Tennessee. That, in turn, engaged Lincoln's deep admiration for the loyal people of this region, effectively serving as a distraction to Lincoln,

Henry Halleck worked as Lt. Gen. Grant's chief of staff and proved a fairly effective administrator. He was one of Lincoln's pall-bearers in April 1865. Halleck is also credited as being one of the people that gave Alaska its name after a visit to that future state. (loc)

James Shackelford commanded the Army of Ohio's newly created cavalry corps; however, he resigned from the service on January 18, 1864 due to the passing of his wife. He passed away in 1909 at his home in Port Huron, Michigan. (aphcw)

who might otherwise be concentrating on other areas. Longstreet had plenty of reasons to loiter in the region.

Longstreet recognized he could have initiated battle at almost any moment. With Parke's infantry lagging behind Shackelford's cavalry, such an opportunity may have presented itself. Shackelford's 4,000 men were somewhat isolated, while Parke's force of about 8,000 men was fourteen miles to the southwest, occupying Rutledge just prior to the opening shots at Bean's Station. "This time was then for full and glorious victory," Longstreet pointed out; "a fruitless one we did not want."

Longstreet directed his commanders in such a manner, perhaps sensing an opening for battle drawing near. He cautioned Brig. Gen. Johnson in their march toward Bean's Station, fearing that the U.S. cavalry might reach that point before Johnson arrived. However, seeing Shackelford isolated, any consideration Longstreet had to simply move into winter quarters vanished, and the battle of Bean's Station took shape.

The history of Bean's Station goes back to the nation's founding. It stood on a vital route toward Cumberland Gap and Knoxville and also the road leading from Knoxville to Virginia. The town consisted of little more than twenty buildings, including a large tavern. Historian Earl Hess noted the small community was in a rolling valley, "north of the Holston River, and a good road ran from the station southwest toward Rutledge, Blain's Crossroads, and Knoxville." The valley at that point, pointed out Capt. Thomas Speed, "is narrow, the mountainsides seeming near at hand. On either side of the village are foothills of the mountains; one hill, in particular, a little southeast of the place commands the approach to the station."

Both sides converged on the little hamlet for the battle of Bean's Station, on December 14, 1863. "I thought to cut off the advance force at Bean's Station," wrote Longstreet, "by putting our main cavalry force east of the river, the other part west of the mountain, so as to close the mountain pass on the west, bar the enemy's retreat by my cavalry in his rear—which was to cross the Holston behind him—then by marching the main column down the valley to capture this advance part of the command [Shackelford]."

Weather, difficult roads, and ill-clad soldiers made Longstreet's approach to the expected battlefield difficult. Porter Alexander commented, "Many of our men were barefooted, and of these numbers failed to keep up with their regiment." Bushrod Johnson echoed similar sentiments in his official report, noting the rise of the Holston River due to the heavy rains.

For the U.S. forces, Shackelford brought twelve regiments of mounted men with him to Bean's Station. Six of the twelve were mounted infantrymen, three of which had fought with William Sanders during his delaying action after Campbell's Station. The 8th Michigan was armed with Spencer repeating rifles. Men of the 24th Kentucky would occupy the tall hotel, turning it into a strong defensive position.

Major General John G. Parke served as Burnside's second in command during the Knoxville campaign. After the war, Parke would serve as superintendent of West Point in the late 1880s. (loc)

Brig. Gen. Bushrod Johnson's 2,600-man division would carry Longstreet's main effort against Shackelford's force at Bean's Station. Johnson's command had reached Rutledge on the 6th of December, remaining there for a few days, making camp at Cloud's Creek from December 9–13. The men were not idle during this period. The want of shoes proved a top priority for Johnson and his men. At Johnson's order, several tanning yards were taken into the Confederates' possession, including several shoe stores. Johnson then put a number of his soldiers experienced as tanners and shoemakers on extra duty "preparing leather and shoes for the men."

Longstreet's double envelopment hinged greatly on his cavalry in the rear. Unfortunately, this part of the plan did not bear fruit. Maj. Gen. Will Martin was to march his command of four brigades and ford the Holston River below the enemy camp. However, he crossed with only a portion of the command and then engaged the enemy at a distance. The other command, under Brig. Gen. William Jones, moving north along the mountains, only looted Federal wagons they came upon and then withdrew. Longstreet commented after the war that Jones "had failed of full comprehension" of the orders as he had directed.

Once in position, Johnson surprised the Federals as the Confederates pressed forward. The U.S. soldiers made strong use of the buildings as they fired to hold Johnson's men back. The hotel—described as one of the finest hotels between New Orleans

Shown here in 1864, the railroad bridge over the Holston River at Strawberry Plains was destroyed and rebuilt four times. (loc)

and Baltimore—proved effective in thwarting the Confederates' advance. Men of the 24th Kentucky poked their weapons through the second and third-story windows, firing into Confederates seeking shelter. Historian Roger Kelley noted, "[f]rom this protected position, [the riflemen] played havoc on the rebel line that advanced toward them." During the assault, Confederate Brig. Gen Archibald Gracie was wounded and had to be removed from the field.

Johnson and his men were not to be denied. Johnson brought forward artillery to within 350 yards of the structure and began to pummel the hotel with solid shot. As holes punched through the walls and explosions resonated inside, the men of the 24th Kentucky made a swift exit through a side door, supported by cavalry as they retreated to safety.

The battle of Bean's Station was effectively over. Maj. Osmun Latrobe of Longstreet's staff called the battle "the briskest little fight of the war."

As the sun faded on the 14th, Porter Alexander located a position at an old graveyard that offered up an entire view of the U.S. position. Alexander did not hesitate to bring his entire battalion forward to take up the position, preparing to rake the entire U.S. line. Longstreet, however, denied Alexander's request to open fire. Longstreet had directed Kershaw's Brigade to strike the enemy's left flank and move into his rear, and he feared Alexander's fire might expose Kershaw's men to danger. Alexander was sorely dismayed. "It was one of the disappointments of my life," he later wrote, "not to have turned my whole battalion loose there that evening."

The Federals pulled back, having sustained just over 100 casualties. However, they had inflicted over 200 casualties on Johnson's command. Still, Longstreet hoped for another opportunity to strike.

Law's and Robertson's brigades had guarded the trains on the 14th, some eight miles away from the battle. Longstreet ordered them up and sent Martin's cavalry to strike up the pursuit. However, Law complained of hardship, and McLaws's men had yet to eat. "There seemed so strong a desire for rest rather than to destroy the enemy," Longstreet bemoaned, "that I was obliged to abandon the pursuit, although the enemy was greatly demoralized and in some confusion. This was the second time during the campaign when the enemy was completely in our power, and we allowed him to escape us." As the Federals withdrew and Longstreet's chance for a fruitful victory evaporated, the Confederate commander concluded, "there was but little opportunity for personal distinction on the part of subordinate officers."

A victory at Bean's Station may very well have provided Longstreet another opportunity to strike at Knoxville, causing Grant in Chattanooga to pause once again on future operations with the persistent Confederates still lingering on his flank. However, with the winter approaching in full force, Longstreet's men, tattered and worn after months of marching and fighting, would settle down into winter quarters.

"A Want of Confidence"

CHAPTER NINE
DECEMBER 1863–APRIL 1864

Just as Longstreet had been one of several disgruntled subordinates serving under Braxton Bragg in the wake of the battle of Chickamauga, he now faced a command crisis of his own. Admidst the frustrations of the Knoxville campaign, the command strains that had simmered in the First Corps all autumn long began to show signs of cracking.

Some of the fault lines, in fact, ran all the way back to the Gettysburg campaign. The seemingly unresolvable issue of who would command Hood's old division continued to fester, although Micah Jenkins continued to hold onto the command. Evander Law had found disfavor from both Jenkins and Longstreet after the disappointments at Wauhatchie and Campbell's Station. Lafayette McLaws came under Longstreet's scrutinizing gaze after the failed assault on Fort Sanders. Lastly, Jerome Robertson, so disgusted with the entire campaign, drifted into

James Longstreet was given command of all Confederate forces in East Tennessee on December 10, 1863. Longstreet maintained his headquarters at the William Nenney House in Russellville, Tennessee, until February 26, 1864, when he moved to Greeneville, Tennessee, closer to the Tennessee and Virginia border. (el)

After leaving Longstreet's Corps, Lafayette McLaws served under Gen. Joseph Johnston in Georgia, attempting to repel the forces under Maj. Gen. William Sherman. (loc)

such a state as to accept only written orders in the future. "These vexations of McLaws, Robertson, and Law showed a weakening, if not a demoralization of Longstreet's command," wrote historian Douglas Southall Freeman.

The relationship between McLaws and Longstreet had gradually deteriorated since Gettysburg, where, per Lee's directives, Longstreet kept a close eye on McLaws's division. The strain on the longtime friendship increased with the McLaws-led assault on Fort Sanders. Longstreet finally relieved McLaws of command on December 17, 1863, placing Brig. Gen. Joseph Kershaw in charge of the division. Longstreet pressed three charges against McLaws. One, McLaws did not position sharpshooters correctly during the assault on Fort Sanders. Second, during the actual assault, McLaws had provided neither proper instruction nor organization to ensure success. Third, McLaws failed to provide any means by which to overcome the enemy's defenses, specifically in crossing the ditch and entering Fort Sanders. When McLaws asked for further clarification on the reasons for the court-martial, Longstreet directed Moxley Sorrel to respond that "you have exhibited a want of confidence in the efforts and plans which the commanding general has thought proper to adopt, and he is apprehensive that this feeling will extend more or less to the troops under your command."

Confederate Secretary of War James Seddon approved the court-martial on January 16, 1864, to be held in Russellville, Tennessee. After a delay, the court convened on February 12 in Morristown, Tennessee. Major General Simon Buckner served as the president of the court. The other members of the court included Maj. Gen. Charles Field and brigadier generals John Gregg, Francis T. Nicholls, George Anderson, Benjamin Humphreys, and James Kemper, who was still recovering from his wounds at Gettysburg and had to make use of crutches. However, military necessity required postponement until the following month.

Meanwhile, McLaws wrote Confederate Adjutant General and Inspector General Samuel Cooper, very much critical of the charges outlined before him. Not thinking himself solely responsible, "I suppose [Longstreet] would have made some mention of

[ladders] at least on some occasion." McLaws stated, "I should think it was his place to order them: his omissions to do neither looks very strange when he charges me with being continually negligent in not getting them."

Once convened, the court found McLaws guilty only of the last charge, failing to provide adequate equipment to overcome the defenses at Fort Sanders. Perplexed by the entire affair, "I had not time or materials, or tools, or any means," a disgruntled McLaws wrote after the battle, "of any kind wherewith to make anything. The commands were without tools of any kind, without axes even, and their wagons and quartermasters were left at Loudon." Nevertheless, the court found McLaws guilty and sentenced him

Joseph Kershaw's office, adjacent to the William Nenney house. Replacing McLaws as division commander, Kershaw led the division through the Overland Campaign and fought Sheridan in the Shenandoah Valley in 1864. Kershaw's troops were captured at the battle of Sailor's Creek just before the war's end. (el)

Currently a private residence, this house served as the headquarters for Brig. Gen. Benjamin Humphreys. Humphreys had taken over the Mississippi brigade when William Barksdale fell at Gettysburg. Humphreys served on the court-martial panel for charges made against some of Longstreet's officers. (el)

to a 60-day suspension of rank and pay. However, Cooper threw out the charges and restored McLaws to command. Despite this exoneration, McLaws would never serve in Longstreet's corps again. In mid-May, he went south to Georgia and supervised the defenses in and around Savannah for the duration of the war.

After the war, Longstreet expressed remorse over the entire McLaws affair. Longstreet even expressed gratitude that Cooper had intervened and relieved McLaws from an embarrassing predicament. Longstreet indicated to McLaws in a July 1873 correspondence that he had relieved McLaws during "an unguarded moment." While there was some reconciliation between the two Confederate warriors, McLaws never truly forgave Longstreet for Old Pete's treatment of him during the months they were in East Tennessee. The entire situation demonstrated the stresses of command Longstreet felt during those cold winter months in East Tennessee. As the saying goes, a command is a lonely place, and Longstreet felt that in the situation with McLaws.

While Longstreet may have reflected some regret about his handling of the McLaws situation, he had no second thoughts about Jerome Robertson. On December 18, Longstreet relieved Robertson when his commander, Brig. Gen. Micah Jenkins, accused Robertson of "conduct highly prejudicial to good order and military discipline." Centered primarily around the battle of Bean's Station, in Longstreet's views, Robertson made comments that, according to Douglas Southall Freeman, indicated "an effort to dodge heavy-duty." Jenkins stated that during the Bean's Station action, Robertson opposed any movement and required written orders, and even then he would obey these orders under protest. To Jenkins, this would inevitably create an atmosphere of distrust and lack of confidence, something neither Jenkins nor Longstreet could tolerate.

Promoted to full general in the Confederate Army in May 1861, Samuel Cooper outranked such Confederate generals as Robert E. Lee, Albert Sidney Johnston, Joseph Johnston, and P. G. T. Beauregard. (loc)

A physician by trade, "Aunt Polly"—as Robertson was known by his men—was much beloved. And the men quickly came to his defense after the same court that heard the McLaws case found Robertson guilty and stripped him from command—a verdict later overturned and replaced with a reprimand. As Texas veteran Benjamin Polley wrote about Robertson:

> *not a member of [Robertson's command] ever blamed him for what he did; on the contrary, the brigade heartily approved of his course, and its survivors are yet grateful to him for the firm stand he took and for the interest and fatherly solicitude he always manifested in the well-being of his men.*

While having no qualms with Brig. Gen. John Gregg, Robertson's replacement, the soldiers of the 4th and 5th Texas Infantry petitioned the officials in Richmond to reinstate Robertson. Soldier testimony recalled Robertson as a "friend" and "one fully able to command the brigade, and at all times willing to sacrifice himself for us and our glorious cause." The petition failed to convince Richmond authorities. Once Gregg recovered from his wound sustained at Chickamauga, he assumed command of the brigade. Confederate authorities shipped Robertson off to Texas, where he commanded the reserve forces in that state.

The final officer to feel Longstreet's wrath was Brig. Gen. Evander Law, the South Carolinian who had led Hood's Division from Thursday, July 2, 1863, until just after Chickamauga in September two months later. Making a note to Longstreet that Lee's "Old Warhorse" had commended him for his performance at Chickamauga, on December 17 Law resigned his position and desired to take his resignation directly to Richmond himself, to which Longstreet offered no objection. Law felt he had been treated unfairly. Both Jenkins and Longstreet placed a large part of the blame for the mishaps at Wauhatchie and Campbell's Station at Law's feet, a charge that Law believed was ill-founded. Law stated a desire to continue his service to the Confederacy in the cavalry. Longstreet approved his leave of absence to Richmond, explaining that "the favor he was doing the service gave him some claim," Longstreet recalled, "to unusual consideration, and his request was granted."

However, Law's departure did not end the drama. With Law in Richmond, Longstreet got wind that the officers in Law's brigade had signed a petition, asking for a transfer to Alabama or Georgia to conduct recruitment duty. Leery of why Law asked to take his resignation personally to Richmond, Longstreet now suspected something was afoul. At the end of December 1863, all but one of the brigade officers submitted a statement corroborating their desire to perform such duty. Furthermore, the petition had nothing to do with Jenkins leading the division or Law having any knowledge of either their intentions or the petition itself. Longstreet determined Law had requested a leave of absence to deceive his commander. For Longstreet, he now had the smoking gun. Longstreet endorsed the officers' petition, forwarding it to Richmond; however, the corps commander was convinced that Law had deliberately tricked him with both the motives and intent behind his leave.

Law never officially submitted his resignation, though. In Richmond, Law met with Maj. Gen. John Bell Hood, who was recovering from his Chickamauga wounds. Hood convinced Law not to carry through his plans. After destroying the document, Law got on a train and returned to East Tennessee on March 1, 1864, where Longstreet promptly had him arrested, charging him with conduct highly prejudicial to good order and military discipline. Longstreet slapped on another charge for conduct unbecoming an officer and a gentleman when he learned that Law had destroyed his resignation paperwork, which Law had written on official Confederate War Department paper.

After the war, Jerome Robertson resumed his medical practice and then entered politics. Robertson held several high positions in the Masons. He died in 1890 at the age of 74. (aphcw)

Meanwhile, authorities in Richmond sought answers regarding Law's case, requesting that Longstreet provide specific charges. Having dealt with the legal procedures for McLaws and Robertson, Richmond now found itself dealing with another problem between Longstreet and a subordinate. However, on April 18, Samuel Cooper decided not to entertain the charges against Law and ordered him restored to command. Richmond had reached the limits of its patience with Longstreet.

In response to Richmond's aversion to holding Law accountable, "I ordered the rearrest of General Law upon his appearance within the limits of the command," Longstreet wrote in his memoirs. "To hold me at the head of the command while encouraging mutinous conduct in its ranks was beyond all the laws and customs of war." It was at this juncture that Longstreet challenged Richmond: either Law must go or else Longstreet had to leave command. Fearful of losing his top subordinate with the spring campaign season not far off, Lee intervened on Longstreet's behalf, urging Richmond to reconsider Law's case. As Morris Penny and J. Gary Laine remarked in their work on Law's Alabama brigade, "it was Lee's opinion that the Confederacy needed Longstreet more than it needed Law."

As the end of April 1864 approached, Law and McLaws collaborated against the First Corps Commander. With both holding grudges against Longstreet, the two conducted what historian Alexander Mendoza called a "two-pronged offensive" against their commander. McLaws would focus his attention on the operations around Knoxville, while Law set his sights on operations around Chattanooga and the pursuit of Burnside up to Knoxville. In the end, however, their efforts fell short when Grant opened up his Overland Campaign on May 5, 1864.

Restored to command in May, Law was with Lee's army only a month before receiving a wound at Cold Harbor on June 3. When he recovered, Law refused to serve under Longstreet and won Lee's approval for transfer to the Confederate cavalry. Law served under Gen. Joseph Johnston during the closing days of the war in 1865.

Less than a year removed from the fields of Gettysburg, three Confederate names well-known to Civil War enthusiasts for their actions during that three-day battle, all subordinates of Lee's "Old Warhorse," now found themselves no longer a part of the Army of Northern Virginia: Lafayette McLaws, Jerome Robertson, and Evander Law. The stresses of a long campaign season, the chronic supply shortages, the lost opportunities, and the actions Longstreet took demonstrated the challenges command brings.

Meanwhile, the issue of who would permanently command Hood's division caused friction within Longstreet's corps for months. Law and Jenkins butting heads was one result of authorities in Richmond failing to decide the issue. On January 16, 1864, Lee wrote Longstreet that "the season of active operations is approaching and I wish the organization perfected." Lee needed a final answer from Richmond before the fighting began. Less than a month later, President Jefferson Davis resolved the lingering issue, naming Maj. Gen. Charles Field to command Hood's division.

A Kentuckian and West Pointer, Field had sustained a serious wound in the August 1862 battle of Second Manassas. Jenkins settled back in command of his old South Carolina brigade. One soldier responded enthusiastically to the news: "All await his return with pleasure and satisfaction as the brigade had had many different commanders and is going to ruin very fast. It will need a commander as General Jenkins to bring it back to its former efficiency and discipline." Unfortunately, Jenkins would not live to see the battle of the Wilderness end, killed during the same incident that wounded Longstreet on May 6, 1864.

Even though a decision had been made, Longstreet was not finished scuffling with Richmond over who would command Hood's division. Upon receiving news that Field would take command, Longstreet instead sought to assign that command to Simon Buckner, directly challenging Richmond's authority on the matter. Cooper, undaunted, replied that was not acceptable. Once again, Longstreet offered up to Cooper and President Davis that Field instead take McLaws's division. With patience all but exhausted, Cooper responded, "[Field] is to take the Division to which he was assigned in orders from this office." Field would go on to command the division for the duration of the war, with some distinction.

Despite Longstreet's ongoing legal imbroglios, there were still military operations to conduct in the winter of 1864. Longstreet would do his best to keep his men fed and clothed while maintaining an aggravating presence to his old friend, Ulysses S. Grant, in East Tennessee.

With Faithful Comrades

CHAPTER TEN

DECEMBER 15, 1863–
FEBRUARY 26, 1864

The area Longstreet and his men occupied "was the most productive part of East Tennessee," concluded historian Oliver Temple. Funneling about twenty miles northeast of Knoxville, the valley was rich and fertile, resting between the Holston and French Broad rivers. Two mountain ranges, the Great Smoky Mountains to the south and the Clinch Mountains to the north, provided safe bookends for Longstreet's command. Longstreet made his headquarters in Russellville, situated strategically near the East Tennessee and Virginia Railroad. From there, Longstreet could maintain limited communications with Richmond.

Longstreet's cavalry set up a wide screen from Rutledge in the north to Dandridge in the south, roughly twenty-five miles in length. The mountain ranges and supporting river networks forced Federal planners to think twice about pursuit of Longstreet, which would give U.S. forces a very narrow avenue of approach through the forty-mile-long valley. Longstreet certainly welcomed the rich lands the valley provided,

The Glenmore Mansion was built on the land where the battle of Mossy Creek occurred. Constructed in 1868-1869, the twenty-seven room, five-story Victorian mansion is considered one of the finest examples of Second Empire-style architecture. (el)

but the strategic and tactical benefits of the terrain might have been even more important. "[F]or those whose mission was strategic," Longstreet concluded, "its geographical and topographical features were more striking."

Despite these operational advantages, Longstreet remained frustrated with the lack of supplies for his men. As temperatures crept slowly toward freezing, many of Longstreet's troops had no overcoats or shoes. The heavy strain of marching took its toll on both men and clothing. Unfortunately for Longstreet, Lee's Army of Northern Virginia took priority for supplies, although even their depots were nearly empty. The inefficient Confederate rail system did not help matters, and engineers worked feverishly to repair broken lines. Brigadier General Micah Jenkins summed it up:

> *I fear that difficulties were increased and the full benefit of well-aimed strategy prevented in this campaign by the absence of high and cordial sustaining support to loyal authority on the part of some high officers, and that the spirit of the army, instead of being encouraged and sustained against sufferings and necessary hardships by some from whom the country had a right to expect it, was, on the contrary, depressed and recognition of dangers and hardships cultivated.*

Longstreet's old friend, Ulysses S. Grant, understood hardships as he traveled to Knoxville at the end of December. Grant arrived to discuss operations with Maj. Gen. John Foster. Even Grant seemed shocked by the temperatures he encountered. "It was an intensely cold winter, the thermometer being down as low as zero every morning for more than a week while I was in Knoxville," Grant later wrote.

While Grant initially favored a more rigorous pursuit, Foster persuaded Grant to hold back. "It would be a good thing to keep Longstreet just where he was," Foster explained, "that he was perfectly quiet in East Tennessee, and if he was forced to leave there, his whole well-equipped army would be free to go to any place where it could effect the most for their cause." Grant concluded this was sound advice and called off strong pursuit of Longstreet.

Looking at it from a slightly different perspective, Lafayette McLaws wrote in his official report that "our force would act as a constant menace upon General Grant's flank and rear, and compel him to keep one equally as large in and about Knoxville to watch our movements." Nevertheless, the Federals looked for opportunities, and one soon emerged at a place called Mossy Creek.

Just a few days before Grant's arrival in Knoxville, Foster's cavalry commander, Brig. Gen. Samuel Sturgis, advanced his 6,000 horsemen to within fifteen miles of Longstreet's encampment. From the area around Mossy Creek, Sturgis got word of a lone Confederate brigade, most likely that of Col. A. A. Russell, near Dandridge to the south. "I determined to take advantage of this division of the enemy's forces and endeavor to surprise and destroy that portion of it," Sturgis wrote in his official report after the battle.

Sturgis ordered the division of Col. John Foster, with elements of Col. Frank Wolford's division, down one road toward Dandridge and the rest of Wolford's command down another road with an "endeavor to surprise and destroy that portion of it." Sturgis also ordered the brigade of Col. Oscar La Grange to be in a position to support either of these forces or Union forces still mustered around Mossy Creek.

Meanwhile, Confederate Maj. Gen. William Martin arrayed his cavalry force on a broad front, believing the U.S. would not operate during such poor weather and with deteriorating road conditions. With the U.S. forces advancing, Martin chose to reinforce Dandridge while also launching an attack against the remaining troopers of Sturgis's command, not far from Mossy Creek, near Talbot's Station. The main action took place near Mossy Creek on December 29, 1863.

While attacking Confederates enjoyed the early momentum, the tide of the battle shifted when reinforcements from Dandridge arrived in the afternoon to bolster Sturgis's command. Sturgis recognized the threat from Martin gathering before him and recalled the elements of La Grange, Foster, and Wolford. By late afternoon, Martin faced a heavy Federal arrangement of cavalry, infantry, and artillery to his front and overlapping both of his flanks. "To advance was impossible," Martin concluded, "and

The battle of Mossy Creek lasted about seven hours, resulting in over 500 casualties for the Confederates and U.S. (el)

to mount and retire on the open fields in daylight before so large a force with such a preponderance of mounted men would, I knew, be difficult."

Captain Eli Lilly's 18th Indiana Battery played a key role in pinning Martin's force in place. Lilly wrote that "my cannoneers were almost completely exhausted by constant labor at the guns on very miry ground, for nearly three hours." When pressed, Lilly changed positions and kept his guns active. The Federal artillery played a decisive role in resisting Martin's advance.

"The Federal advance toward Longstreet's winter encampment had been halted," historian Roger Kelley wrote, "as had the Confederate move toward Mossy Creek."

*   *   *

This latest setback capped what may have been Longstreet's nadir in the war. Laying out a rather depressing outlook, biographer Jeffry Wert described

Lee's "Old Warhorse" as a man "broken by the burdens of independent command, by the knowledge of his failures at Lookout Valley and at Knoxville; he was a general without direction and a man without self-assurance."

With Federal pressure mounting near his headquarters and the internal discord of his command gaining visibility, Longstreet felt a change of command was necessary. Writing to Samuel Cooper on December 30, 1863, Longstreet shouldered the blame for the missed opportunity represented by the Knoxville campaign. "And I desire, therefore, that some other commander be tried," he concluded. "I believe this is the only personal favor that I have asked of the government, and I hope that I may have reason to expect that it may be granted."

Longstreet's request was ultimately denied, and he remained in service in East Tennessee. He resigned to "stay and go down with faithful comrades of long and arduous service," he wrote in his memoirs.

*   *   *

Two weeks later and with temperatures plummeting, Longstreet found himself positioned for another potential engagement against Federal troops. As with Sturgis's original movement, this opportunity was near the fertile grounds of Dandridge, astride the French Broad River. The rich foraging areas around Dandridge appealed to both Confederates and U.S. forces. The icy conditions on the rivers made transporting supplies from Chattanooga for Foster's men challenging. Obtaining the area around the French Broad River offered an appealing objective for the Federals. Longstreet recognized it, as well, for the same reasons. In addition, Longstreet described the terrain as "bold and inviting for military work."

Major General John Parke commanded in place of Foster, who was ill. Armed with three cavalry divisions led by Sturgis, Parke also had three infantry divisions under the command of Gordon Granger. The operational objective was to gain a firm grip on the foraging areas around Dandridge, "keep[ing] the enemy as far from the city as possible and to subsist your men and horses." Furthermore, they would

Shortly after the battle of Mossy Creek, Union officer Eli Lilly transferred to the cavalry. His unit was captured by Nathan Bedford Forrest in Middle Tennessee, and Lilly remained a prisoner for most of the remainder of the war. After the war, wanting to preserve life versus take it, in 1876, Lilly's small drug store in Indianapolis grew into the Eli Lilly Pharmaceutical Company, still meeting the needs of customers today. (ihs)

protect the foraging parties as they scattered across the countryside.

Granger could, as necessary, construct ferries across the French Broad River to assist in his foraging operations. Keeping in mind the soldiers settled in Knoxville, Granger would "also collect all possible subsistence and forage more than for need of your own command, this excess of supplies to be sent in boats to Knoxville."

Longstreet was quick to respond to Union movements toward Dandridge. By mid-afternoon on January 15, he had more than sixty-one infantry regiments—the divisions of Brig. Gens. Micah Jenkins and Bushrod Johnson—twenty pieces of artillery, and eighteen regiments of cavalry on the roads toward Dandridge. As Longstreet wrote later, the soldiers "were prepared to do their share towards making an effective battle, and our plans were so laid."

The 125th Ohio Infantry, known as the "Opdyckes Tigers," found themselves in this swale, pinned down by Confederate sharpshooters during the fight around the town of Dandridge. It was not until darkness came that they were able to withdraw, though still under sporadic Confederate fire. (el)

Minor skirmishes occurred on both January 16 and 17. The Union forces arrived at Dandridge first, setting up a perimeter around the town; however, the Union commanders did not anticipate an encounter with Longstreet's infantry. Hoping to get in the rear of Parke's forces, Longstreet recalled, "the flank movement was handsomely executed, and it was handsomely followed by the dismounted infantry." Based upon Longstreet's movements, Parke rethought his strategy on the evening of January 17.

Complicating matters for Parke was an error made by Maj. Gen. Phil Sheridan. Sheridan had built a bridge over the French Broad for the purpose of gaining a position below Dandridge and supervising the construction of a pontoon bridge; however, to his dismay, the bridge only covered part of the river. Sheridan mistook "the large area of land on Fain's Island for the opposite bank of the river and constructed his bridge upon the island." Parke concluded it would take up to four hours to finish the bridge. Meanwhile, Longstreet was pressing heavily on his forces in and around Dandridge. "Our loss was severe, considering the short duration of the affair," Parke concluded in his official report.

With Sheridan's error along the French Broad and mounting losses when pressed by Longstreet, the approach of bad weather heightened Parke's anxiety for future operations. Consequently, he held a Council of War with his commanders and senior staff on the evening of January 17. Erroneously, Parke received word that Longstreet had been reinforced. With all these matters to consider, Parke chose to withdraw

On the attic walls of the Fairview Mansion in Gallatin, Tennessee, one can still detect the names in candle smoke of many U.S. Army soldiers, reflecting their occupancy in this house during the war. The mansion is currently a private residence. (el)

In the parlor of this small house in Dandridge, James Longstreet and his staff made a toast to Major General Granger. Granger had apparently left a bottle of alcohol on the table before his departure. (el)

back toward Strawberry Plains, building fires to mask his movements.

As Union forces withdrew, Longstreet and his staff moved into Dandridge. In the town, a lady came out of her small store and invited them into her parlor. Longstreet and his staff obliged, relieved to get out of the unpleasant weather. The lady presented to Longstreet a bottle that she stated had belonged to Maj. Gen. Gordon Granger, who had left it there from the previous evening when they had elected to withdraw from the area, much to Granger's disgust. The woman mentioned she had never heard a person swear about another person as Granger did that evening. The whiskey flask had about two inches of liquid left and the Confederate officers did not want to waste it. Longstreet concluded the story in his memoirs: "Colonel Fairfax, who knew how to enjoy good things, thought the occasion called for a sentiment, and offered, 'General Granger—may his shadow never grow less.'" Hampered by the deteriorating conditions and weather, Longstreet's pursuit fell short.

Longstreet wrote to Lee on February 2 stating that bad weather made it almost impossible to trail the enemy and that his force "could only pursue with our cavalry." The Confederates gained some arms and ammunition, left behind by Parke's men. "Our infantry," Longstreet recalled, "was not in condition to pursue, half of our men being without shoes. Our cavalry is almost as badly off for want of clothing, and the horses are without shoes, or nearly half of them."

Though minor in nature, the action at Dandridge protected, for some time, Longstreet's hold on the only foraging country in reach.

The Union made additional efforts on the foraging grounds around Dandridge on January 27, this time moving south of the French Broad River. Longstreet left behind the infantry division of Brig. Gen. Bushrod Johnson and Martin's cavalry to keep an eye on things. "The enemy, by a rapid movement, threw his cavalry around through Knoxville into Sevier County, for the purpose of occupying the only foraging county in reach," Longstreet explained to Lee on February 2. "Our cavalry was ordered to cross the river in his rear and cut off his force, which, in his demoralized condition, was thought proper." However,

Sites in Dandridge, Tennessee

Arrow Hill Mansion

Helen Topping Miller's 1954 book, *No Tears for Christmas*, a novel set in the winter of 1863 in East Tennessee, had Arrow Hill Mansion as its inspiration. Helen wrote, "History to me, however, is not a mere chronicle of dates and battles, but a vivid story of people—their struggles, loves, and hates, their frustrations and disappointments, their dreams and victories." (el)

in Longstreet's eyes, Martin's execution of the orders was slow and "our ranks were broken in confusion."

The maneuvering at Fair Garden continued on the next day at Kelley's Ford. "On the morning of the 28th I moved my whole command toward the French Broad River, on the direct road from Fair Garden to Dandridge, with the view of engaging the enemy's cavalry where it might be found," wrote Samuel Sturgis in his official report. Hard marching and fighting also sapped the strength of the Union soldiers and their mounts. Sturgis concluded, "we could not live here and fight Longstreet's infantry."

Sturgis did go after Armstrong's cavalry division before the infantry could close up. However, a strong stand by Longstreet's cavalry allowed Bushrod Johnson's men to threaten the Union rear. "The battle lasted until sundown, when, finding the infantry in our rear advancing, I withdrew to this place by way of Fair Garden," Sturgis recounted. Longstreet could finally boast that the Union withdrawal "left us in possession of the foraging grounds."

Soon, however, Longstreet was left with very few horse soldiers. On February 20, Bragg, now in Richmond, reassigned most of Martin's cavalry

Sites in Dandridge, Tennessee (cont.)

The Shepard Inn

The Shepard Inn was built around 1814. This popular resting and eating spot for stage coach travelers has entertained three U.S. Presidents: Andrew Jackson, James K. Polk, and Andrew Johnson. (el)

to Gen. Joseph Johnston's Army of Tennessee. Longstreet was left with only two cavalry brigades, under the command of Cols. Arthur Russell and George Dibrell. This limited Longstreet's ability to scan the fields around his command for Federal movements. Though Longstreet made a slight advancement against Knoxville in early February, the absence of cavalry severely impacted his capability to gather intelligence.

"The prime object," Longstreet wrote in his memoirs, "was to show the strategic strength of the field, and persuade the authorities that an army of twenty thousand in that zone could be of greater

The Revolutionary War Graveyard

At the original site of the Hopewell Presbyterian Church, organized in 1785, the Revolutionary War graveyard contains the graves of some early citizens and Revolutionary War veterans. (el)

service than double that force on the enemy's front or elsewhere." Writing to Lee on February 22, Longstreet stated, "This makes it necessary that I should withdraw my forces to a point in my rear with less exposed flanks than in my present position, and will take me so far back and leave me so little cavalry, that I can hope to do nothing more than wait for the enemy to turn me out by one flank or the other, and throw me gradually back."

A few days later, on February 26, Longstreet moved his headquarters further toward Virginia, to Greeneville, Tennessee, in what would be the last chapter of his East Tennessee campaign.

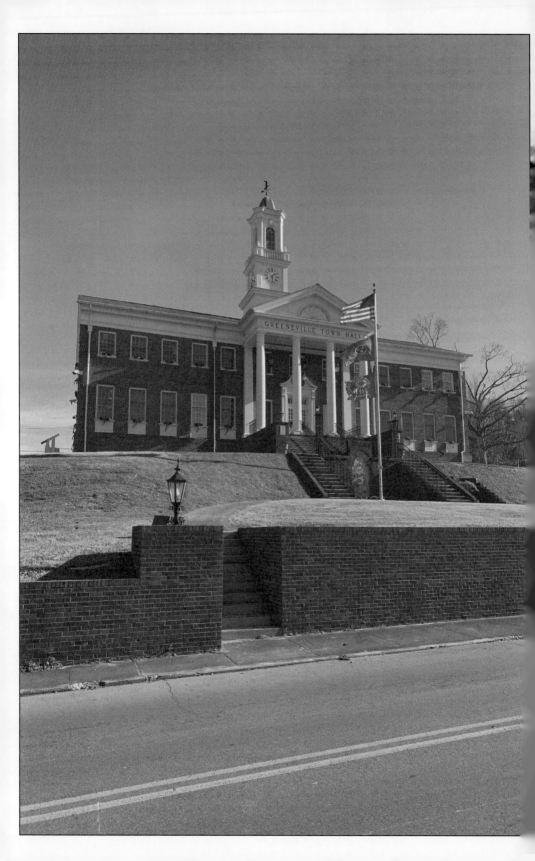

"Carry Me Back to Old Virginia"

CHAPTER ELEVEN
FEBRUARY 27–APRIL 29, 1864

As far back as mid-December 1863, the soldiers under Longstreet's command took notice of the harsh weather that often buffeted them. Writing to his wife on December 18, young Alexander McNeil commented the "army is very poorly prepared for this weather as quite a number of them are barefooted as well as poorly clad." One soldier from the 13th Mississippi Infantry Regiment recalled that, out of 300 soldiers in the regiment, only 32 were reported to have shoes available. As a result, soldiers marched "with their feet bleeding at every step."

The quick departure from Virginia seemingly a lifetime ago in September 1863 now bore consequences as soldiers who lacked winter gear and fresh shoes struggled with the cold weather. Even Longstreet commented that the last days of 1863 and into January 1864 were some of the coldest days of the war, with the thermometer consistently falling below zero. One Georgia soldier summed it up nicely when he wrote that East Tennessee, with all its deprivations

On February 28, 1864, Longstreet moved into the home of Unionist Samuel Milligan, a judge who lived in Greeneville, Tennessee. The Greeneville Town Hall now occupies the site. (el)

and severe weather, "truly is a world of forgetfulness." A myriad of factors interrupted Longstreet's supply chain. By early 1864, the Union controlled vast swaths of southern land that had previously helped feed Southern armies. The fall of Vicksburg and Port Hudson in the summer of 1863 cut off these same armies from western livestock. The blockade off southern coastlines thwarted efforts to receive supplies from overseas. The often-inconsistent operations of railroad systems only stressed the already delicate Southern transportation network. And a centralized procurement system did not help matters. The entire Confederate economy was showing strains. Historian James McPherson pointed out, "The rampant inflation that plagued the Confederate economy also made farmers reluctant to sell at government rates, which were invariably lower than market prices."

For Longstreet, in the distant reaches of the Confederacy, the need to supply his army stretched the quartermaster's talents. Often, supplies had to be filtered through Lynchburg, Virginia, and then sent forward along the damaged Virginia and East Tennessee Railroad. Lee grew so concerned with this logistical nightmare that he recommended that the Confederate authorities end Longstreet's East Tennessee campaign and send him back to Virginia. "A major Confederate army of almost 20,000 men," stated historian Harold Wilson, "dangled at the end of a supply line almost 1,000 miles long." As Wilson pointed out, Lee's Army of Northern Virginia drew almost twice the quantity of supplies and goods as they had the previous year—so much so that sustaining Longstreet's army became extremely challenging.

As snow and cold temperatures penetrated the bivouacs of Longstreet's soldiers, the men got innovative in their approaches to survival. Chasing rabbits became a regular activity, promoting a good deal of fun in addition to the prospect of a good meal. One group of soldiers found themselves in a grove of sugar maple trees. They noticed the sap was beginning to run down the trees. The soldiers gathered up the sap, strained it into their canteens through handkerchiefs, and ended up with a tasty syrup.

The deprivations and sense of hopelessness in East Tennessee caused many soldiers to seek an escape

American Civil War Museum

from their situation. Longstreet's corps saw increasing desertions during the cold winter days of 1863-1864. "Boredom, cold, hunger, separation from loved ones, and the awareness of great valor and suffering apparently wasted, all weighted down on them through the early months of 1864," stated historians Warren Wilkinson and Steven Woodworth. In his address to the Confederate Congress on February 4, 1864, Jefferson Davis feared that "desertion, already a frightful evil, will become the order of the day." As an example, historian Susannah Ural, writing on Hood's Texas Brigade, noted that 20 percent of the 102 courts-martial in the brigade took place during the East Tennessee campaign. In the sturdy and usually reliable Texas Brigade, only 6 percent of soldiers deserted during the war; however, 34 percent of those desertions took place while the brigade operated in East Tennessee.

For soldiers from Arkansas or Texas, Union control of the Mississippi River only increased their stress, being so far from home and now finding communication with family all the more difficult.

Taken in Huntsville, Texas, the survivors of Hood's Texans assemble. (acwm)

Andrew Johnson in Greeneville, Tennessee

Home and Burial Place of President Andrew Johnson

Greeneville, Tennessee, is the home of the nation's 17th President, including two of his homes, his tailor shop, and his gravesite. Pictured are one of Johnson's homes in Greeneville (above), his gravesite at Andrew Johnson National Cemetery (left), and a statue of Johnson near the visitor center of the Andrew Johnson National Historical Site (right). (el)

John Hunt Morgan in Greeneville, Tennessee

The Death of General John Hunt Morgan

Construction began on the Dickson-Williams Mansion in 1815 and was completed in 1821. Catharine Dickson married Dr. Alexander Williams in 1823 and entertained many guests in the mansion, some said to include Marquis de Lafayette; Presidents Andrew Johnson, Andrew Jackson, and James K. Polk; the famous Frontiersman Davy Crockett; and statesman Henry Clay. In September 1864, the "Thunderbolt of the Confederacy," Gen. John Hunt Morgan, spent his last night alive in the mansion. The Lexington Cemetery in Kentucky is Morgan's final resting place. (el)

Grant opens his Overland Campaign, fighting his way through the battle of the Wilderness in early May 1864. (loc)

Deficient rail systems and an inadequate supply system prolonged the frustration soldiers bore in East Tennessee. As historian Frank Vandiver underscored, "the problems of all the war department supply agencies were similar: procurement, transportation, and distribution." Longstreet's command felt the effects of all three throughout his stay. And as if supply problems weren't enough for Longstreet's beleaguered troops, fighting off Union patrols and pro-Union bushwhackers increased the stress for both soldiers and leadership.

During his last weeks at his headquarters in Greeneville, Tennessee, when he was not concentrating on procuring food and supplies for his men and horses, Longstreet looked to advance his views on Confederate strategy. He persuaded Robert E. Lee to back some of his ideas, bringing them to President Jefferson Davis. However, it was all for naught. As Longstreet later wrote, "[President Davis and his cabinet] could not or would not hear of plans that proposed to take them from the settled policy of meeting the enemy where he was prepared for us."

With diminished cavalry support and intelligence that units from East Tennessee were headed to the Eastern Theater, on April 7, 1864, after a long, frustrating, cold winter, Longstreet received orders to rejoin the Army of Northern Virginia. Invariably whenever bands struck up a tune, "Carry Me Back to Old Virginia" always generated the largest response. Even the thought of heading into Virginia "added spring in their step," said one soldier, which "made the trip all the more easy."

In the post-Civil War years, Robert E. Lee and James Longstreet maintained a friendly and cordial friendship. The attacks against Longstreet's reputation and integrity commenced after Lee died in October 1870. (acwm)

Unfortunately, difficulties still followed Longstreet's command. While in Bristol, Virginia, on April 5, heavy snow fell, ten to twelve inches deep. With food already scarce, the town had few provisions for the men. So, they stormed the local commissary and carried away seventy-five to eighty sacks of flour and several hundred pounds of bacon, at the cost, unfortunately, of several wounded and two soldiers killed. Nonetheless, for both officers and soldiers, "after seven unhappy and disastrous months in Georgia and Tennessee, they were, once again, back in Virginia."

Escaping the scorn and penetrating looks that Longstreet's men endured in pro-Union East Tennessee was an added relief to all. Writing his sister on April 22, 1864, Capt. John Jeffries reflected, "I am made to feel more thankful than ever before for being spared when so many have fallen around me; and they as good or better than me, and have a fair prospect at the beginning to come through safe as I have." One soldier even commented on the welcome reception from Virginia ladies waving their handkerchiefs as they rolled into the state that "created all the enthusiastic effects of the first year of the war."

Lee could not withhold his enthusiasm at having Longstreet back under his command. "I really am beside myself, General, with joy of having you back," Lee wrote to Longstreet on April 29. "It is like the reunion of a family." Lee felt the occasion warranted a grand review of the army, which took place a few miles south of Gordonsville, Virginia. This was truly a special occasion; Lee hadn't held a grand review since after the battle of Antietam in September

1862. With the resources they had, the soldiers went to great lengths to make their appearance suitable for their beloved Robert E. Lee—"an acceptable display before our commander in chief," wrote one Confederate soldier.

The review on April 29 was indeed a grand spectacle. The soldiers formed in double columns, the artillerists firing their cannons in salute of their commander and their army. Hundreds of flags fluttered through the air; hats and caps littered the ground, tossed about when their commanders rode past. Augustus Dickert recalled it took several hours for the units to pass in review. Soldiers remarked how "Generals Lee and Longstreet were very pleasant and chatty, smiling, and talking." Burdened for months with empty stomachs and elusive victories while in East Tennessee, one soldier saw hope for the future: "We were all strengthened in our confidence in complete success when we beheld our able leader looking so well."

That opportunity presented itself when Lt. Gen. Ulysses S. Grant's Overland Campaign began just a few days later.

As both Longstreet and Lee prepared for another spring campaign, Longstreet may have had opportunity to reflect on the joint resolution the Confederate Congress had passed on February 17, 1864. The Congress applauded:

> *their patriotic services and brilliant achievements in the present war, sharing as they have the arduous fatigues and privations of many campaigns in Virginia, Maryland, Pennsylvania, Georgia, and Tennessee, and participating in nearly every great battle fought in those states, the commanding general ever displaying great ability, skill, and prudence in command, and the officers and men the most heroic bravery, fortitude, and energy, in every duty they have been called upon to perform.*

Perhaps Longstreet did take comfort in that resolution passed by the authorities in Richmond. Or, maybe, Longstreet recalled those few key words relayed in a message sent to Braxton Bragg on November 11, 1863, as the march on Knoxville was just beginning.

Longstreet might have looked back at the setback that was Fort Sanders or reflected on the strained supply system and bitter cold that confronted his army. The decisions made against senior officers in his command surely did not reflect a sense of satisfaction from Lee's "Old Warhorse."

Yet, going back to that November message, he might have just shaken his head at how it all played out, from Chickamauga to when he rejoined Lee's Army of Northern Virginia. Longstreet could have simply uttered, "another fine opportunity lost."

Epilogue

The spring fighting season opened in early May 1864. Newly minted with the rank of lieutenant general and general-in-chief for the U.S. armies, Longstreet's old friend, Ulysses S. Grant, moved forward in the Eastern Theater in what came to be known as the Overland Campaign. General Robert E. Lee sought safety and security for his Army of Northern Virginia within the maze of dense woods of the Wilderness. Lee hoped to offset Grant's superiority in almost every facet of organization.

On May 6, back under Lee's command, Longstreet pushed forward along the Plank Road in pursuit of retreating U.S. forces. Unfortunately, the same fate that befell Lt. Gen. "Stonewall" Jackson almost a year earlier struck once again.

Longstreet and his small entourage found themselves between units, out front, and dangerously exposed. As the chaos and confusion of battle grew

Longstreet's postwar conflicts with fellow Confederates would leave him written out of much of Southern histories of the war. Even in the Wilderness, where Longstreet turned the tide of battle on the second day before being grievously wounded, his crucial role in the battle was ignored in favor of other stories that reinforced a more romanticized version of events. (cm)

Longstreet's wounding occurred during the battle of the Wilderness in May 1864. Longstreet's flanking force advanced perpendicular to the Orange Plank Road, the 12th Virginia Infantry part of that element. A small forest fire split the organization as it moved forward. Working to consolidate, soldiers of the command fired upon Longstreet's small party. Micah Jenkins was killed and Longstreet severely wounded. (nps/ecw)

stronger, some Confederates noticed Longstreet's party, mistaking them for U.S. soldiers, and immediately opened fire. Longstreet took a bullet to his throat, which passed through his right shoulder. Brigadier General Micah Jenkins received a bullet to the head, killing him instantly.

"The blow lifted me from the saddle," Longstreet remembered, "and my right arm dropped to my side, but I settled back to my seat, and started to ride on, when in a minute the flow of blood admonished me that my work for the day was done."

Longstreet survived the wound; however, Lee would be without his "Old Warhorse" for a number of months. Longstreet would not return until Lee and Grant had settled into a stalemate during the siege at Petersburg.

Upon his return to Lee's army in October 1864, Longstreet and Lee continued together throughout the remaining months of the war. A determined Longstreet still resolved to hope. When Lee asked him, in early April 1865, whether should they receive Grant's demands for surrender, Longstreet firmly replied, "Not yet." However, not long after, Lee surrendered to Grant at Appomattox, with the war concluding a month later with Gen. Joseph Johnston's surrender at Bennett Place.

Historian and Longstreet biographer Jeffry Wert captured Longstreet's legacy throughout the war: "He neither viewed war as a moral absolute, like Jackson, nor accepted the effectiveness of the tactical offensive, like Lee. He advocated strategic audacity and tactical conservatism. He preferred to spare men's lives rather than test their character. An attack without strategic purpose or without the chance of tactical success violated the principles of his generalship."

Unfortunately, Longstreet's same audacity and tactical acumen on a battlefield fell short during the highly politically charged post-Civil War years. The vigorous pursuit by Lee's worshippers to restore their benevolent leader's reputation and standing in the South gained strength after Lee's death in October

Longstreet lost many of his personal belongings, including items from the war, during a house fire. He died in Gainesville, Georgia, just a few days short of his 83rd birthday. (tslc)

1870. As part of that crusade, they set their sights on James Longstreet.

Two years after Lee's death and on the anniversary of his birth—January 19, 1872—one of Lee's commanders, Jubal Early, jump-started the offensive against Longstreet with a speech at Washington and Lee University in Lexington, Virginia. Early's comments pointed to Longstreet's performance at the battle of Gettysburg in July 1863, accusing Longstreet of being late. One year later, Lee's old artillery chief, William N. Pendleton, poured more fuel on the fire, introducing the famous sunrise order at Gettysburg, which Lee allegedly directed for Longstreet to execute on July 2, 1863.

It is telling that Early and Pendleton waited until after Lee's passing before launching salvoes in Longstreet's direction. Arguably, Lee would not

James Longstreet died on January 2, 1904, and is buried in Gainesville, Georgia. A funeral procession occurred four days after his death and included the Queen City Band, Candler Horse Guards, governor's Horse Guards, Confederate veterans, family, and friends. (ds)

have tolerated any such attacks against his trusty subordinate. These critics, Early and Pendleton in particular, "apparently sought to win in peacetime, as defenders of Lee," noted historian William Garrett Piston, "the reputations that had eluded them during the war. By blaming Longstreet for the Confederacy's failure to win independence, they drew attention away from their own shortcomings." Longstreet spent years and expended much energy striving to restore his reputation and standing.

During the years following the Civil War, referred to commonly as Reconstruction, Longstreet took positions oftentimes at odds with many in the South. He saw submitting to the decisions made for Reconstruction as one of the more peaceful options that would better the South in the long run. In other words, the South should concede to the principles laid out by the Republican Party—almost unheard of with many strong Democrats throughout the South. But as Wert explained, Longstreet saw it as an accommodation until a restoration of power could take place; that is, he urged cooperation until such time as leaders could once again control the South and the black vote.

James Longstreet shouldered other characteristics that put him at odds with the Lost Causers in the South. Along with maintaining close ties with Ulysses S. Grant, Longstreet accepted a Federal position in New Orleans. His wife, Louise, passed in late December 1889. Eight years later, Longstreet married a much younger Helen Dortch, a native of Georgia and strongly devoted to her Catholic faith. Longstreet converted to Catholicism. The association with the Republican Party and the Catholic Church did not endear the former general to most of his former Southern colleagues.

Longtime Civil War-era historian Eric Foner points out that when Longstreet died in January 1904, the United Daughters of the Confederacy did not adorn his gravestone with flowers. Aside from a diminutive and tucked-away statue at Gettysburg, one would have to look far and wide to find any statues dedicated to the service and memory of James Longstreet in the South. They simply don't exist—all evidence to the positions Longstreet took after the war and, perhaps, more impactfully, the means and measures others took to run his reputation into the ground.

Civil War Knoxville and the Loss of Fort Sanders

APPENDIX A

BY JIM DONCASTER

1890 was a banner year for Civil War reconciliation and remembrance. In August of that year, the United States Congress authorized the establishment of the first National Military Park to preserve and protect the battlefields at Chickamauga and Chattanooga. Two months later and a hundred miles away, 10,000 Civil War Union and Confederate veterans gathered in Knoxville for one of the earliest of the Blue-Gray Reunions. The year marked the 25th anniversary of the end of the war and the 27th anniversary of the battle of Fort Sanders where many of them had met on the field of battle. They were there now "to remember and to forget," as one speaker said in the spirit of reconciliation, "to remember the heroic deeds and the mighty works of the past . . . and to forget all else."

Forgetting was made easier by the post-war transformation of the city. Gone were most of the defensive works that Capt. Orlando M. Poe had meticulously laid out in a protective ring around the town, lost to urban expansion. Fort Sanders, the linchpin of the fortifications, was not exempt. The Reunion's commemorative medallion captured what would soon be its fate. One side of the medal contained an image of Fort Sanders under assault, and the other the inscription "Its Memory Alone Remains."

The front view of the Deaf and Dumb Asylum in Knoxville, now the present site of the Lincoln Memorial University Duncan School of Law. (jd)

Memorials, Monuments, and Cemeteries

The UDC Confederate Monument

Fort Sanders was lost, but what the brave men North and South did there was not to be forgotten. In 1914, the Knoxville Chapter of the United Daughters of the Confederacy (Chapter 89) installed on 17th Street near the corner of Laurel Avenue a marble monument to the Confederate soldiers who died in the battle nearby. The monument contains a short poem along with the dedicatory inscription: "To the memory of the Confederate soldiers who fell in the Assault on Fort Sanders, November 29, 1863."

The 79th New York "Highlanders" Monument

A monument dedicated to the 79th New York "Highlander" Infantry Regiment. Fittingly for the call of reconciliation, the monument has a U.S. and Confederate soldier shaking hands. The monument is located at the intersection of 16th Street and Clinch Avenue in Knoxville. (el)

Four years later and two blocks away at the corner of 16th Street and Clinch Avenue, the state of New York erected a marble monument to its sons who served in the 79th New York "Highlander" regiment defending Fort Sanders. Reflecting the spirit of the time, the monument includes a bas relief of a Union and a Confederate soldier shaking hands and a poem to reconciliation.

The National Cemetery and the Union Soldiers Monument

Major General Ambrose Burnside established the Knoxville National Cemetery in 1863, securing a final resting place for over 9,000 veterans. (va)

Fitting for a city with divided loyalties and one held by both armies at different times, Knoxville has both a National and a Confederate Cemetery. The National Cemetery at 939 Tyson Street was established in 1863 by order of General Ambrose E. Burnside shortly after his arrival in the city. Laid out in "wagon wheel" fashion, the cemetery was to become the final resting place of more than 3,000 Union soldiers, including those from Fort Sanders, by war's end. Today more than 9,000 veterans are buried in the cemetery, including several soldiers who served in the U.S. Colored Troops and one lone Confederate.

A marble monument to the Union soldiers buried in the National Cemetery was unveiled in 1901. Atop the monument was a bronze eagle perched upon a cannonball. In 1904 a lightning bolt struck the eagle, shattering it and severely damaging the monument below. An eight-foot marble Union soldier crowned the monument when it was unveiled a second time in 1906.

Bethel Cemetery and
the Confederate Soldiers Monument

Two miles east of the National Cemetery at 1917 Bethel Avenue is the Confederate Cemetery, or Bethel Cemetery as it is formally known. There at war's end the remains of 1,600 Confederate soldiers were reinterred from other sites around Knoxville along with the remains of fifty Union soldiers who are believed to have died in Confederate captivity. Initially tended by the Ladies Memorial Association of Knoxville, the cemetery is now maintained by the Mabry-Hazen House and Museum but has fallen on hard times.

Two prominent features of Bethel Cemetery that do remain in good condition are the Confederate Monument and the bronze tablets to the Confederate dead. The former, the first Civil War monument erected in Knoxville, was dedicated in 1892. The tall marble monument with a vigilant Confederate sentry atop was designed and sculpted by Knoxville's own Lloyd Branson. The bronze tablets inscribed with the names of many of the Confederate dead, including those killed or mortally wounded at Fort Sanders, were added in 1961.

Mount Olive Cemetery and
the Sultana Monument

There are only a few monuments in the country to the Sultana, the steamboat that exploded and sank in the flooded Mississippi River just north of Memphis in the closing days of the Civil War. One of those monuments is in Knoxville's Mount Olive Cemetery at 2507 Old Maryville Pike. The boat was filled with paroled Union soldiers, many of them from East Tennessee. An estimated 1,200 men died in what is considered the greatest maritime disaster in United States history. The monument was dedicated in 1916 after funds were raised by a Knoxville Sultana Survivors organization. It contains the names of those Tennesseans known to have died in the disaster along with totals from other Northern states.

Noteworthy Homes and Edifices

More than forty antebellum houses and buildings remain in Knox County today. Among the many that played a significant role in the Civil War, and specifically in the Knoxville campaign and the Battle of Fort Sanders, are the eight listed below.

Crescent Bend
2728 Kingston Pike

Built in 1834 by Drury Armstrong, this home was the headquarters of Confederate General Joseph Kershaw during the siege of Knoxville. As such it was the closest headquarters to the front lines during the siege and attack on Fort Sanders. Today the home is a museum owned by the Toms Foundation and open to the public.

Built in 1834, the Armstrong House served as the headquarters for Brig. Gen. Joseph Kershaw throughout the siege of Knoxville. It is also known as Crescent Bend for its positioning near a bend on the Tennessee River. (el)

A plaque on the side of the Bleak House tells the tale of part of the house's service during the opening engagements outside Knoxville (el)

Bleak House
3148 Kingston Pike

Bleak House was the headquarters of commanding Lt. Gen. James Longstreet and Lt. Gen. Lafayette McLaws during the siege of Knoxville. Built by Robert Houston Armstrong, the son of Drury Armstrong, the house was occupied by Confederate troops during the prelude to the siege as they tried to dislodge a makeshift line of Sanders's dismounted cavalry several hundred yards in advance on November 17 and 18, 1863. Now known as Confederate Memorial Hall, the home is owned and operated by the United Daughters of the Confederacy and open to the public by appointment.

The Knollwood home overlooks the route that both U.S. and Confederate forces took when entering Knoxville. It was briefly occupied by James Longstreet after the battle of Campbell's Station and the early days of the siege in November 1863. (jd)

Knollwood
6411 Kingston Pike

This majestic house atop Bearden Hill overlooks the route taken by Maj. Gen. Burnside and Lt. Gen. Longstreet into Knoxville. Longstreet occupied this house after the Battle of Campbell's Station and in the initial days of the siege. The home has since been converted into offices and is not open to the public.

Baker-Peters House
9000 Kingston Pike

Dr. Harvey Baker, a Confederate sympathizer, was killed in the Baker Peter's house, now a restaurant. (jd)

Constructed in 1830 by Dr. Harvey Baker, the home was occupied by Dr. Baker, a Confederate sympathizer, until his death at the hands of Union cavalrymen under the command of then Col. William Sanders during a June 1863 raid. Dr. Baker allegedly was killed by a bullet fired through a barricaded door, a door that remains in the house today and evinces signs of the struggle. The Baker House is now the site of Finn's Restaurant and Tavern.

Lamar House (Bijou Theatre)
803 South Gay Street

The most significant building downtown during the Civil War was the Lamar House. The hotel housed Federal and Confederate soldiers at various times during the war, including Confederate Gen. Joseph E. Johnston, and it was the center of social activities for both armies. Union Cavalry commander Brig. Gen. William Sanders was brought to the Lamar House after his mortal wounding, and he died there soon after. Today the Lamar House is home to the Bijou Theatre and the Bistro at the Bijou restaurant.

Mabry-Hazen House
1711 Dandridge Avenue

Knoxville businessman Joseph Mabry's house stood on a high hill east of town. The home was the headquarters of Confederate commanding Brig. Gen. Felix Zollicoffer before he was killed at Mill Springs in January 1862. During the Union occupation of the city, the rifle pits and redoubt at Mabry's Hill marked the eastern end of Orlando Poe's defensive line.

Blount Mansion
200 West Hill Avenue

The only mansion in Knoxville designated as a National Historic Landmark is the Blount Mansion. Belle Boyd, the Confederate spy, stayed in this mansion in the summer of 1863. (jd)

Just down the street from the Bijou Theatre (Lamar House) is the oldest house in Knoxville, Blount Mansion. Built in 1792 for then territorial governor William Blount, the mansion was the home of the Boyd family during the Civil War. The notorious Confederate spy Belle Boyd stayed at the house in the summer of 1863 after her clandestine activities had been discovered by federal authorities in Virginia. The mansion, which is the only Knoxville building designated a National Historic Landmark, is open to the public.

Deaf and Dumb Asylum
601 West Summit Hill Drive

What is now Lincoln Memorial University's Duncan School of Law was formerly the Tennessee School for the Deaf. Before and during the Civil War it was called the Deaf and Dumb Asylum. During the war's first two years, it became the primary site for treating sick and wounded southern soldiers and was labeled simply "Asylum Hospital." The name was retained by the Union forces who used it for the same purpose after their move into Knoxville in September 1863.

Now part of a law school, the Deaf and Dumb Asylum Hospital became a primary location for wounded soldiers. U.S. soldiers labeled it as the "Asylum Hospital" when they occupied Knoxville. (jd)

Then & Now

While most of the major action in and around Knoxville occurred north of the Tennessee River— the Battle of Campbell's Station on November 16, Sanders's delaying action on the Kingston Pike on the 17th and 18th, and of course the climatic assault on Fort Sanders on the 29th – the areas south of the river were not without conflict. As Longstreet and Burnside maneuvered above the river, Maj. Gen. Joseph Wheeler, with portions of four brigades of cavalry, was dispatched by Longstreet to make a southern approach to Knoxville via Maryville. Contesting their advance were elements of Sanders's cavalry, who fought delaying actions near Rockford and Stock Creek before being driven back into the city on the 15th. Only the presence of Union infantry supported by artillery on the hills south of the river kept Wheeler from crossing the pontoon bridge in pursuit. Heavy skirmishing on the 15th and 16th occurred on the lower heights of what would soon become Forts Dickerson and Stanley and in the valley between them.

The most significant action south of the river occurred on November 25, when Robertson's and Law's Confederate brigades, the same brigades that had fought at Gettysburg's Little Round Top less than five months before, clashed with Cameron's blocking brigade of Union infantry. After scores of casualties were inflicted on both sides, the attacking Confederates returned to their lines on Cherokee Heights. Burnside and Poe examined the field and assessed the continuing threat the next day. The result was the creation of a battery position with supporting infantry trenchwork on a neighboring hill christened "Fort Higley."

Due to the topography of the land south of the Tennessee River, sites important to the contending armies generally have not suffered the fate of those north of it. The rugged hills opposite town rise from the southern riverbank to eminences more than three hundred feet in height, stymying contemporary development. Not all the land of historical significance there has been preserved, but much of it has thanks to the ongoing efforts of the City of Knoxville, the Aslan Foundation, and the Legacy Parks Foundation, with support from the American Battlefield Trust and the Knoxville Civil War Round Table. Because of the varying involvement of the different groups in the preservation efforts, the hills and crowning forts and fortifications will be addressed individually. Moving from west to east, they are Cherokee Heights, Armstrong Hill, Fort Higley, Fort Dickerson, and Fort Stanley.

Preservation South of the River

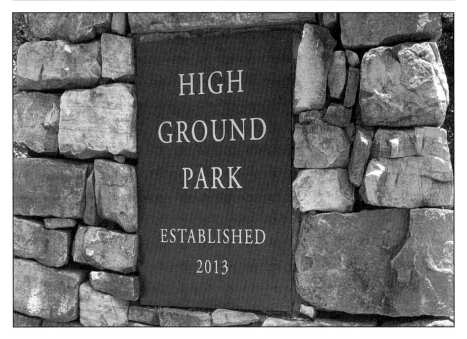

Cherokee Heights (Cherokee Bluff)

The lower slopes of Cherokee Heights on the eastern side from which Law and Robertson launched their attack on Cameron's brigade are as rough and wooded now as they were in 1863 and are totally undeveloped. The flat top of the bluff above these slopes, where artillery commander E. Porter Alexander trained the guns of Captain William Parker's Virginia battery on the federal lines across the river, sadly was lost to development in the late twentieth century. A gated condominium village now occupies this once lofty Confederate position.

Armstrong Hill

Drury Armstrong owned the parcel of land that bore his name and became the site of the largest fight of the Knoxville campaign south of the river. The land, accessible by the Cherokee Trail today, remained in private hands for the next 150 years until it was purchased by Legacy Parks Foundation in 2009. According to Carol Evans, Executive Director

High Ground Park is located at 1000 Cherokee Trail in Knoxville. The one-mile trail takes one past rifle trenches and a cannon enclosure, part of the defensive network that was Fort Higley. (el)

of Legacy Parks, the foundation raised $1.5 million, including a $10,000 donation from the American Battlefield Trust, to acquire the River Bluff property, which encompasses Armstrong Hill. Legacy Parks then deeded the property to the City of Knoxville in November of 2015 for inclusion in Knoxville's Urban Wilderness. Hiking trails and interpretive signage on the Armstrong Hill fight are currently under study by the city and the foundation.

Fort Higley

After the fight at Armstrong Hill, Burnside and Poe thought it expedient to strengthen the western edge of the city's southside defenses. U.S. troops emplaced guns from Fort Stanley and dug infantry trenchwork in a figure 8 pattern in what soon would be called Fort Higley. No significant action occurred in this sector after these defensive moves were made. Fort Higley remained in private hands well into the twenty-first century. When condo developers began eying the site, the Aslan Foundation intervened in 2008, purchasing a 39-acre tract that held the fort. After archeological work was conducted at the site, Aslan developed the area into a public park that opened in 2013. Today High Ground Park, which remains under Aslan's stewardship, contains abundant signage and well-maintained trails that lead to the old earthen fort, an old Military Road, and overlooks with sweeping vistas of the area. The park is accessible via the Cherokee Trail and is open to the public daily according to the foundation's Executive Director Andrea Bailey.

Fort Dickerson

By far the best-preserved remnant of the Civil War in Knoxville is Fort Dickerson. Begun in the days leading up to the siege to protect the southern approaches to the city and completed in February 1864, after the siege was lifted, the fort remains the best example of a Civil War earthen fort in East Tennessee. The fort remained in private hands until it became an 85-acre city park in 1957. Fort Dickerson was the site of a large centennial reenactment of the Battle of Fort Sanders in 1963, and it has been the site

of annual reenactments and living history weekends conducted by the Knoxville Civil War Round Table for almost forty years. Over the years, the fort has been gradually restored by the Round Table and the City of Knoxville. Trees and vines have been removed, viewsheds opened, and three artillery pieces were purchased and placed in the fort's embrasures by the Round Table to approximate the look of the fort

Fort Dickerson was the first and most potent of the four earthworks that U.S. engineers built on the heights south of the Tennessee River across from Knoxville. (el)

Fort Dickerson is the only remaining fort of Burnside's defenses in the Knoxville area during the Civil War. Just opposite the opening of the Second Creek, it lies west of present-day Chapman Highway. (el)

in wartime. The Aslan Foundation in 2017 created a beautiful new Fort Dickerson Gateway to welcome visitors entering the park at 3000 Fort Dickerson Road off Chapman Highway. Aslan also has been funding kudzu removal in the park and is making plans to build boardwalks beneath the ramparts of the fort to protect its earthen walls.

Fort Stanley

The hill upon which Fort Stanley sits is just to the east of Fort Dickerson across present-day Chapman Highway. Together the two forts commanded the approaches to the city from the south. Union trenchwork and rifle pits defined Fort Stanley during the siege, and afterwards tents covered hillsides cleared to provide fields of fire. Today, little of Fort Stanley remains, and what does exist is vine-covered and overgrown. Nevertheless, the Aslan Foundation purchased 22 acres of the hill in 2011 to protect the site and is considering purchasing additional acreage to protect the viewshed from the city.

The Future

One of the most enticing features of life in Knoxville today is the development of the Knoxville Urban Wilderness. According to the Visit Knoxville website, "Knoxville's Urban Wilderness is a spectacular outdoor adventure area where you can hike, bike, climb, paddle, or just wander in the woods—all within the heart of the city. Over 50 miles of trails and greenways connect you to a beautiful nature center, pristine lakes, historic sites, dramatic quarries, adventure playgrounds, five city parks, and a 500-acre wildlife area."

The Urban Wilderness master plan calls for the forging of a new series of trails called the "Battlefield Loop." The loop trail as proposed would link the Armstrong Hill battlefield with Forts Higley, Dickerson, and Stanley—in effect connecting all the extant Civil War sites south of the river. Much of the trail already exists, though some connecting links are yet to be defined. Still, thanks to the visionary thinking of leaders in city government, area foundations, and local civic organizations, the future for historic preservation, restoration, and interpretation in Knoxville never looked brighter. The Battlefield loop was not even a pipe dream twenty years ago. Soon it will be a reality.

JIM DONCASTER *is a former president of the Knoxville Civil War Round Table.*

HEADQUARTERS
ARMY OF TENNESSEE,
GENERAL BRAXTON BRAGG,
SEPT. 20TH, 1863.

James Longstreet and the Army of Tennessee's High Command

APPENDIX B

BY CECILY NELSON ZANDER

Many Civil War historians would consider it an understatement to say that Braxton Bragg had a difficult personality. This was especially true in late 1863, when the Army of Tennessee's high command seemed at its breaking point, despite having just won their first true victory in the battle of Chickamauga. The triumph over William Starke Rosecrans did little to assuage doubts among many of Bragg's subordinates about their commanding officer, however. The weeks following the successful fight along the Georgia-Tennessee border, noted Confederate artillerist (and native Georgian) Edward Porter Alexander, featured camps rife with dissatisfaction in Bragg's army. "Very few" of the Army of Tennessee's high-ranking officers, Alexander wrote, "were sanguine of any success under [Bragg's] leadership." Tensions ran so high after the battle that Confederate president Jefferson Davis left Richmond to visit the feuding commanders in person.

The command situation, already populated by some of the war's most querulous personalities, had been further complicated by the arrival of Lt. Gen. James Longstreet and the Army of Northern Virginia's First Corps at the end of September. In the days following the battle of Gettysburg, Gen. Robert E. Lee predicted

Braxton Bragg's command problems began in earnest in the wake of Stones River. By the time Longstreet arrived at the battle of Chickamauga, the situation had deteriorated significantly. Longstreet waded into the thick of the controversy. (cm)

Braxton Bragg assumed command of the Army of Tennessee in the summer of 1862. He had consistent problems with subordinate commanders throughout his time in command. (loc)

A close Longstreet confidant, Senator Louis Wigfall was a strong advocate for the "Western Policy" approach. (loc)

that the Army of the Potomac would be "as quiet as a sucking dove" for at least six months, despite its victory over his own army. As that prediction proved true, the men of Lee's army sat idle in their camps near Culpeper, Virginia. Meanwhile, Bragg abandoned the vital railroad junction of Chattanooga, Tennessee, and retreated into the mountains of northwestern Georgia. President Davis asked Lee whether he might be willing to transfer a portion of his force to help Bragg out of his predicament. The Virginian offered to send Longstreet's First Corps to reinforce the beleaguered Bragg.

Longstreet's arrival irrevocably changed the dynamic in Bragg's army. Before proceeding, it is important to keep three facts in mind:

1. Even before his arrival in Tennessee, Longstreet doubted Bragg's competence as a commander, writing to Texas senator Louis T. Wigfall on August 18 that Bragg lacked the ability to command an army.

2. Within days of his attachment to Bragg's army, Longstreet denounced Bragg as incompetent in a September 26 letter to Confederate Secretary of War James Seddon, despite receiving Bragg's praise for his part at the victory at Chickamauga six days prior.

Longstreet became the de facto leader of the anti-Bragg faction following the battle of Chickamauga. His relationship with Bragg quickly deteriorated as operations in Chattanooga commenced. (aphcw)

3. On October 4, Longstreet joined with ten senior officers in Bragg's army and lent his stature to an anti-Bragg petition, sent to President Davis requesting that the Confederate Commander-in-Chief replace Bragg with a more suitable commander.

It is no wonder, then, that while reflecting on the close of the momentous year of 1863, Confederate brigadier general and Army of Tennessee observer William Whann Mackall informed Joseph Johnston: "I think Longstreet has done more injury to the general [Bragg] than all the others put together."

Longstreet did not relish the idea of serving under Bragg. Before setting foot outside of Virginia, in fact, he wrote to Richmond suggesting "putting me in General Bragg's place." Without any firsthand experience of life in Bragg's army, Longstreet further asserted: "I doubt if General Bragg has great confidence in his troops or himself either." Old Pete, it seemed, had already made up his mind about Bragg. When he found that he would not be superseding the Army of Tennessee's longtime commander, he joined with the cabal of officers who appeared to spend more time fighting Bragg behind the scenes than they did fighting the Union forces in their front. None of these men could boast illustrious battlefield careers—Longstreet was by far the most successful of the lot—

Bragg's attempt to starve William Rosecrans into submission in Chattanooga failed when General Grant assumed overall command and re-opened U.S. supply lines. (na)

but Leonidas Polk, Daniel Harvey Hill, Simon Bolivar Buckner, Alexander P. Stewart, Joseph Wheeler, and several others felt justified in leveling complaints against their commander.

The reasons for their discontent varied—but seemed to stem from the belief that Bragg was not the man to lead them to victory. After all, the general had notable shortcomings as a combat commander. According to historian Thomas Lawrence Connelly, Bragg was "dull, sour, pedantic," and "did not seem to understand people." The North Carolinian was further hurt by "his constant fear of making a mistake and his consequent hesitation in committing his troops." He did not understand the value of terrain. He "always looked for infringements on his prerogatives by his superiors and for infractions of rules by his subordinates." T. Harry Williams called him "probably the ugliest and most disliked Southern general." Bragg quarreled continuously with many of his generals, and the quarrels consumed both his time and energy. By late 1863, Bragg had been so battered by internal and external criticism that historian Richard M. McMurry suggested he "was suffering from the beginnings of a nervous and physical breakdown." And the arrival of Longstreet didn't ameliorate Bragg's condition.

Longstreet joined the partisans aligned against his commanding officer almost immediately following the victory at Chickamauga. Old Pete explained to Secretary of War James Seddon that Bragg had no sense of how to lead an army or fight a battle. "To express my convictions in a few words, [Bragg] has done but one thing he ought to have done since I joined his army," wrote Longstreet on September 26, 1863. "That was to order the attack upon the 20th. All other things that he has done, he ought not to have done. I am convinced that nothing but the hand of God can save us or help us as long as we have our present commander." Three days later, Longstreet used his influence to persuade eleven other members of the Army of Tennessee's high command, including three division commanders, to sign a petition demanding that President Jefferson Davis remove Bragg from command of the army.

Though the army's anti-Bragg faction had grown steadily since the retreat from Kentucky following the battle of Perryville in 1862, it was not until Longstreet's arrival that the aggrieved subordinate officers requested removal of their commander. Whatever motives may have generated Longstreet's revolt against Bragg—one historian has suggested that Longstreet coveted the command of the Army of Tennessee for himself and had an axe to grind— he had enough prestige to convince a significant number of officers to form a cabal. And, perhaps more critically, Longstreet had enough standing in Richmond that President Davis proved willing to entertain the complaint, which, under military law amounted to an act of insubordination on the part of Longstreet and his cohorts.

The revolt may have taken Bragg by surprise, as he did his best to accommodate Longstreet's arrival and to encourage the new addition to his army. On the first night of the battle of Chickamauga, Bragg altered the command structure of his army specifically to accommodate Longstreet. He reorganized the

The Confederacy had five secretaries of war during the war, with James Seddon serving the longest from 1862-1865. U.S. forces arrested him in May 1865, and he served seven months in prison, retiring from public service after his release. (loc)

A bishop in the Episcopal Church, Lt. Gen. Leonidas Polk quarreled frequently with Braxton Bragg, who removed Polk from command after the battle of Chickamauga. (aphcw)

army into two wings, one commanded by Longstreet and the other by Leonidas Polk, his most senior lieutenant. Lt. Gen. D. H. Hill, while he retained corps command, resented Polk's elevation over him to wing command, which the North Carolinian considered a "needless affront."

Following the victory at Chickamauga, Bragg acknowledged Longstreet's leadership as prompt, vigorous, and satisfactory. Though Longstreet received Bragg's commendation after Chickamauga, he remained frustrated that Bragg did not follow up the victory by pursuing the Federal troops then entrenching in Chattanooga. On multiple occasions after the battle, Longstreet claimed that Bragg discarded his advice with little, if any, consideration. A bitter correspondence in the battle's aftermath regarding the Union army's newly established cracker line indicated that neither Bragg nor Longstreet would accept the blame for failing to consolidate their victory. Bragg held Longstreet personally responsible, through his inactivity and half-heartedness, for the establishment of the Federal cracker line; Longstreet blamed Bragg for failing to promptly approve a battle plan that would have prevented the Federals from establishing the line in the first place.

Before Jefferson Davis visited the Army of Tennessee in the autumn of 1863, he admitted privately that he had no intention of removing Bragg from command, despite the fervent requests of Longstreet and the subordinate cabal. At Bragg's headquarters, Davis called a meeting of the corps and division commanders to discuss the army's future. The meeting opened with a discussion of strategy but degenerated into a lambasting of Bragg. Longstreet excoriated Bragg's leadership and called for his removal, a recommendation seconded by Cheatham, Hill, and others. But Davis sided with Bragg, issued a public statement of support for him, and returned to Richmond. The entire affair constituted one of the most bizarre military scenes of the war. Bragg, apparently "a little confused," listened to his subordinates speak against his leadership while the president of the Confederacy determined not to pay any heed to the complaints. As if to underscore how strange the event had been, Davis neglected to mention it in his two-volume memoirs of the war.

There can be little doubt that the arrival of James Longstreet turned scattered and individual objections to Bragg's leadership into a collective effort to remove the Army of Tennessee's commander. At no point, before, during, or after his service with Bragg did Longstreet give any indication of respect for his commander. Longstreet's brief time in the Army of Tennessee lifted the lid on a pot of roiling discontent. Though he contributed substantively to the army's victory at Chickamauga, he made no subsequent effort to work with Bragg. The two went their separate ways to defeat: Bragg at Chattanooga and Longstreet at Knoxville. There is little doubt that the Confederate forces would have made a more successful effort if the two senior commanders had been able—or willing—to work together.

CECILY NELSON ZANDER *is Emerging Civil War's chief historian. She is an assistant professor at Texas Women's College.*

Longstreet and Confederate Strategy

APPENDIX C

BY ED LOWE

As the May 1863 battle of Chancellorsville raged, James Longstreet and two of his divisions had been detailed off in search of supplies and food in the Suffolk area, reuniting with the rest of the Army of Northern Virginia in time for the Gettysburg campaign. Even before Gettysburg, Longstreet proposed uniting with the command of Gen. Joseph Johnston in Mississippi and assuming the offensive against Rosecrans and his Army of the Cumberland, perhaps forcing Grant's hand and relinquishing his aim at Vicksburg. And after the September battle of Chickamauga, Longstreet once again proposed to cross the Tennessee River and pressure Rosecrans's grip on Chattanooga. Lastly, Longstreet made a projection for a move into Kentucky. The primitive Confederate logistical system made all three options all but impossible. However, these examples do illustrate Longstreet's strategic thinking, looking beyond his own area of operations.

As historian R. I. DiNardo and Albert A. Nofi suggest, Longstreet's vision went "well beyond the parochial concerns of so many of his contemporaries."

As seen from Fort Negley, modern downtown Nashville still embodies Tennessee's political, commercial, and cultural influence. In February 1862, it became the first Confederate capital to fall during the war—a major blow to the Confederacy. U.S. forces occupied the state of Tennessee for the duration of the war. (cm)

The battle of Nashville, December 15-16, 1864, proved a significant victory and arguably the most decisive tactical victory by either the U.S. or the Confederacy during the entire war. (aphcw)

One could make a case that even Robert E. Lee could not see beyond his own blinders—Virginia, and his beloved Army of Northern Virginia. Longstreet at least could look at both theaters, making recommendations on what he thought was best for the Confederacy at the time.

Bracing for the coming winter while in East Tennessee, Longstreet wrote Adjutant General Cooper on December 13, 1863. Forward thinking, Longstreet proposed that "if we regain possession of East Tennessee, I think that our position here against the enemy's flank, in case he attempts to move into Georgia, will be a good one, and it will be a good point from which we may threaten the enemy's rear in Kentucky and at Nashville." Mounting his command on horses and mules, Longstreet hoped to replicate similar efforts seen during the war, with a force running roughshod in the enemy's rear, breaking up railroads and disrupting supply operations. And military considerations aside, the political consequences of a successful effort might reverberate in the presidential elections, less than a year away. As Longstreet biographer Jeffry Wert explained, "the stakes necessitated the risks, a gamble against the long odds and the deepening darkness moving toward the Confederacy. It was the judgment of a general with strategic insights." However, authorities in Richmond vetoed the idea for the primary reason that they considered it impossible to sustain such an operation with sufficient animals and forage.

Longstreet certainly recognized the challenges caused by the steady decline of logistical support from the Confederate government to plan and then execute strategy. "I do not see how they can be overcome," Lee wrote to Longstreet on February 17, 1864, with respect to Longstreet's suggestions.

Nashville was significant to both the U.S. and the Confederacy as a major shipping and rail center. (loc)

As part of an overall Confederate strategy in 1864, Longstreet envisioned Joseph Johnston (above) pulling his troops out of Alabama and Mississippi to augment Longstreet's command for operations across Tennessee and then into Kentucky. (loc)

Recognizing such limitations, President Davis recommended that Longstreet link up with Gen. Joseph Johnston, who had replaced Bragg in command of the Army of Tennessee on December 27, 1863, in order to disrupt the enemy's lines of communications between Chattanooga and Nashville, perhaps even moving into Kentucky as conditions developed. Yet, even Johnston demurred on such action. "The attempt to unite the Army of Tennessee and Longstreet's corps, near Kingston," Johnston wrote in his memoirs, "would be a violation of a sound military role, never to assemble the troops that are to act together, in such a manner that the enemy's army may attack any considerable body of them before their union." Even bringing Gen. P. G. T. Beauregard's forces into the mix from Charleston proved impracticable for logistical challenges. "Where Longstreet's planning was original, it was not practical, and where it was practical it was not original," concluded historian Douglas Southall Freeman.

Even if the Richmond leadership rejected Longstreet's suggestions, his presence in East Tennessee could still serve a legitimate purpose: as a deterrence to U.S. movements. As the spring 1864 fighting season began, Longstreet in East Tennessee could have influenced Sherman's advance against Johnston's Army of Tennessee near Dalton, Georgia. Yet even this was not to be, as Davis recalled Longstreet back to Lee's Army of Northern Virginia in time for the battle of the Wilderness in May 1864. Writing in his memoirs, Longstreet lamented: "[T]he authorities could not be induced to abandon the policy of placing detachments to defend points to which the enemy chose to call us. We had troops enough in Tennessee, Georgia, Alabama, and Mississippi, if allowed to use them in cooperative combination, to break the entire front of the Federal forces and force them back into Kentucky before the opening of the spring campaign, when we might have found opportunity to 'dictate' their campaign. The enemy was in no condition for backward move at the time of my advance upon Knoxville, so simultaneous advance of our many columns could have given him serious trouble, if not confusion."

Again, perhaps, another lost opportunity.

Longstreet recommended bringing 20,000 troops under Gen. P. G. T. Beauregard (above) by rail to Virginia and then having them march into Kentucky. (aphcw)

James Longstreet passed away in 1904. This home in Gainesville, Georgia, was his last residence. It is now the Winner Wellness Center. His memoirs, written late in life and after many contemporaries could no longer contest them, made assertions about his role in Confederate command decisions that remain controversial. (sr)

Order of Battle

KNOXVILLE CAMPAIGN

UNION FORCES
Department and Army of the Ohio
Maj. Gen. Ambrose Burnside

NINTH CORPS: Brig. Gen. Robert B. Potter
FIRST DIVISION: Brig. Gen. Edward Ferrero
First Brigade: Col. David Morrison
36th Massachusetts • 8th Michigan • 79th New York • 45th Pennsylvania

Second Brigade: Col. Benjamin C. Christ
29th Massachusetts • 27th Michigan • 46th New York • 50th Pennsylvania

Third Brigade: Col. William Humphrey
2nd Michigan • 17th Michigan • 20th Michigan • 100th Pennsylvania

Artillery
Battery L, 2nd New York Light Artillery • Battery D, 1st Rhode Island Light Artillery

SECOND DIVISION: Col. John F. Hartranft
First Brigade: Col. Joshua K. Sigfried
2nd Maryland • 21st Massachusetts • 48th Pennsylvania

Second Brigade: Lt. Col. Edwin Schall
35th Massachusetts • 11th New Hampshire • 51st Pennsylvania

Artillery
15th Battery, Indiana Light Artillery • Co. E. 2nd U.S. Artillery
Batteries L and M, 3rd U.S. Artillery

TWENTY-THIRD CORPS: Brig. Gen. Mahlon D. Manson
SECOND DIVISION: Brig. Gen. Julius White
Second Brigade: Col. Marshal W. Chapin
107th Illinois • 13th Kentucky • 23rd Michigan • 111th Ohio
Henshaw's Light Battery, Illinois

THIRD DIVISION: Brig. Gen. Milo S. Hascall
First Brigade: Col. John W. Reilly
44th Ohio • 100th Ohio • 104th Ohio • Battery D, 1st Ohio Light Artillery

Second Brigade: Col. Daniel Cameron
65th Illinois • 24th Kentucky • 103rd Ohio • Wilder Battery, Indiana

Reserve Artillery: Capt. Andrew J. Konkle
24th Indiana Battery • 19th Ohio Battery

Provisional Brigade: Col. William A. Hoskins
12th Kentucky • 8th Tennessee

CAVALRY CORPS: Brig. Gen. James M. Shackelford
FIRST DIVISION: Brig. Gen. William P. Sanders/Col. Frank Wolford
First Brigade: Col. Frank Wolford/Lt. Col. Silas Adams
1st Kentucky • 11th Kentucky • 12th Kentucky

Second Brigade: Lt. Col. Emery S. Bond
112th Illinois (mounted infantry) • 8th Michigan • 45th Ohio (mounted infantry)
15th Indiana Battery

Third Brigade: Col. Charles D. Pennebaker
11th Kentucky (mounted infantry) • 27th Kentucky (mounted infantry)

SECOND DIVISION: Col. John W. Foster
First Brigade: Col. Israel Garrard
2nd Ohio • 7th Ohio • 2nd East Tennessee (mounted Infantry)

Second Brigade: Col. Felix W. Graham
14th Illinois • 5th Indiana • 65th Indiana (mounted infantry) • Colvin's Illinois Light Battery

CONFEDERATE FORCES
Longstreet's First Corps
Lt. Gen. James Longstreet

MCLAWS'S DIVISION: Maj. Gen. Lafayette McLaws
Kershaw's Brigade: Brig. Gen. Joseph B. Kershaw
2nd South Carolina • 3rd South Carolina • 7th South Carolina • 8th South Carolina
15th South Carolina • 3rd South Carolina Battalion

Wofford's Brigade: Col. Solon Z. Ruff; Lt. Col. N. L. Hutchins, Jr.
16th Georgia • 18th Georgia • 24th Georgia • Cobb's Georgia Legion
Phillips Georgia Legion • 3rd Georgia Battalion Sharpshooters

Humphreys's Brigade: Brig. Gen. Benjamin G. Humphreys
13th Mississippi • 17th Mississippi • 18th Mississippi • 21st Mississippi

Bryan's Brigade: Brig. Gen. Goode Bryan
10th Georgia • 50th Georgia • 51st Georgia • 53rd Georgia

HOOD'S DIVISION: Brig. Gen. Micah Jenkins
Jenkins's Brigade: Col. John Bratton
1st South Carolina • 2nd South Carolina • 5th South Carolina • 6th South Carolina
Hampton South Carolina Legion • Palmetto South Carolina Sharpshooters

Robertson's Brigade: Brig. Gen. Jerome B. Robertson
3rd Arkansas • 1st Texas • 4th Texas • 5th Texas

Law's Brigade: Brig. Gen. Evander M. Law
4th Alabama • 15th Alabama • 44th Alabama • 47th Alabama • 48th Alabama

Anderson's Brigade: Brig. Gen. G. T. Anderson
7th Georgia • 8th Georgia • 9th Georgia • 11th Georgia • 59th Georgia

Benning's Brigade: Brig. Gen. Henry L. Benning
2nd Georgia • 15th Georgia • 17th Georgia • 20th Georgia

ARTILLERY: Col. E. Porter Alexander
9th Georgia Artillery Battalion, Companies C, D

Alexander's Battalion: Maj. Frank Huger
Moody's Louisiana Battery • Fickling's South Carolina Battery • Jordan's Virginia Battery
Parker's Virginia Battery • Taylor's Virginia Battery • Woolfolk's Virginia Battery

BUCKNER'S DIVISION: Brig. Gen. Bushrod R. Johnson
Gracie's Brigade: Brig. Gen. Archibald Gracie, Jr.
41st Alabama • 43rd Alabama • 59th Alabama • 60th Alabama

Johnson's Brigade: Col. John S. Fulton
17th Tennessee • 23rd Tennessee • 25th Tennessee • 44th Tennessee • 63rd Tennessee

Cavalry Corps: Maj. Gen. Joseph Wheeler/Maj. Gen. William T. Martin
MARTIN'S DIVISION: Maj. Gen. William T. Martin
First Brigade: Brig. Gen. John T. Morgan
1st Alabama • 3rd Alabama • 4th Alabama • 7th Alabama • 51st Alabama

Second Brigade: Col. J. J. Morrison
1st Georgia • 2nd Georgia • 3rd Georgia • 4th Georgia • 6th Georgia

ARMSTRONG'S DIVISION: Brig. Gen. Frank C. Armstrong
First Brigade: Brig. Gen. William Y.C. Humes/Col. George G. Dibrell
4th Tennessee • 8th Tennessee • 9th Tennessee • 10th Tennessee

Second Brigade: Col. C. H. Tyler
Clay's Kentucky Cavalry Battalion • Edmundson's Virginia Cavalry Battalion
Jessee's Kentucky Cavalry Battalion • Johnson's Kentucky Cavalry Battalion

WHARTON'S DIVISION: Brig. Gen. Gabriel C. Wharton
First Brigade: Col. Thomas Harrison
3rd Arkansas Cavalry • 65th North Carolina (6th Cavalry) • 8th Texas Cavalry
11th Texas Cavalry

Artillery
Freeman's Tennessee Battery • White's Tennessee Battery • Wiggins's Arkansas Battery

Suggested Reading

A FINE OPPORTUNITY LOST

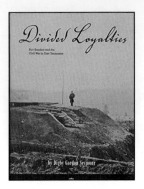

Divided Loyalties: Fort Sanders and the Civil War in East Tennessee
Digby Gordon Seymour
East Tennessee Historical Society, 2002
ISBN-13: 978-0941199131

A detailed study and analysis of the operations around Knoxville in fall of 1863. The seminal work on the assault of Fort Sanders, Seymour provides an excellent narrative along with maps and photographs. Seymour captures the importance Burnside's defense at Knoxville played in this pivotal moment of the Civil War. Any student of the operations around Knoxville must put *Divided Loyalties* in their library.

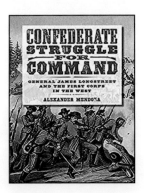

Confederate Struggle for Command: General James Longstreet and the First Corps in the West
Alexander Mendoza
Texas A&M University Press, 2008
ISBN-13: 978-1603440523

Mendoza's book provides a good overview of Longstreet's East Tennessee Campaign. In particular, he provides an excellent summary of Longstreet's legal challenges in the winter of 1863 with some of his top commanders. A worthy companion to any book that explores this part of the Civil War.

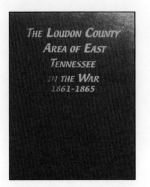

The Loudon County Area of East Tennessee in the War, 1861–1865
Gerald L. Augustus
Turner Publishing Company, 2000
ISBN-13: 978-1563116872

Written by a local historian, Augustus's book is rich in its story telling and full of interesting facts. It provides a strong context for Longstreet's continued journey to Knoxville and the East Tennessee Campaign. A very focused area read for this part of America's Civil War.

*The Knoxville Campaign: Burnside and Longstreet in
East Tennessee*
Earl J. Hess
University of Tennessee, 2013
ISBN-13: 978-1572339958

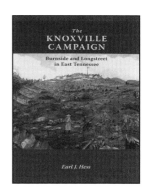

As with the other works of Earl Hess, you'll find
this work also fulfilling. A strong addition to
the Civil War historiography that provides the
reader immense context for how Longstreet's East
Tennessee Campaign and Ambrose Burnside's
stance at Knoxville shaped the remaining years of
America's Civil War.

*Where Men Died: Little Known Battlefields of the American
Civil War*
Roger Campbell Kelley
CreateSpace Independent Publishing Platform, 2012
ISBN-13: 978-1479346776

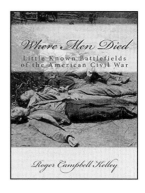

A wonderfully charming book, full of interesting stories
and facts. A quick read that covers some of Longstreet's
key engagements during the East Tennessee campaign.
If you want a quick overview of this campaign, grab
Kelley's book. You won't be disappointed.

*Battle of Bean's Station: Last Battle of Longstreet's Knoxville
Campaign, 1863*
Donald Sheridan
CreateSpace Independent Publishing Platform, 2020
ISBN-13: 978-1548436827

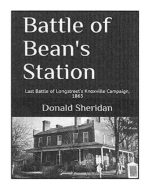

Sheridan's focused work on this battle is a must
on any Civil War bookshelf, especially regarding
Longstreet's East Tennessee Campaign. Along with
the narrative, the book provides fascinating pictures
of Bean's Station both before the war and after the
majority of the battlefield went under water.

About the Author

Col. Ed Lowe (USA, Ret.) served 26 years on active duty in the U.S. Army, with deployments to Operation Desert Shield/Storm, Haiti, Afghanistan, and Iraq. He attended North Georgia College and has graduate degrees from California State University Dominguez Hills, the U.S. Army War College, U.S. Command & General Staff College, and Webster's University. He is an adjunct professor for the University of Maryland/Global Campus and Elizabethtown College, where he teaches history and government. He resides in Ooltewah, Tennessee, with his wife, Suzanne, and has two daughters, Sarah and Robyn. Sarah is married to U.S. Army veteran Travis Miller.